the new avant-garde

*This book is dedicated
to the memory of Alan Solomon*

Praeger Publishers, Inc.
111 Fourth Avenue, New York, N. Y. 10003, U.S.A.
5 Cromwell Place, London S.W.7, England

Published in the United States of America in 1972
by Praeger Publishers, Inc.

Library of Congress Catalog Card Number: 72-166514

Printed in Italy by Edizioni d'Arte Alfieri.

the new avant-garde

Issues for the Art of the Seventies

Text by Grégoire Müller
Photographs by Gianfranco Gorgoni

Praeger Publishers
New York · Washington · London

PERCEPTION CAN NEVER BE DISSOCIATED FROM KNOWLEDGE, FROM MEMORY, AND FROM THE ACTUAL LOCATION IN THE TIME AND THE SPACE OF ITS OCCURENCE.
DIFFERENT ELEMENTS FORM IN TURN A NEW MEANING BEYOND THE FAIRLY OBVIOUS MEANINGLESSNESS OF THE PIECES; IT IS THE LANGUAGE OF REALITY ITSELF.

Grateful acknowledgement is made to the following individuals: Marianne Barcellona, Leo Castelli, Virginia Dwan, Tina Girouard, Richard Landry, Barbara Lipper, Claude Picasso, Mark Radclif, Ivan Della Tana, John Weber, and Barbara Wool.
Photographs on pages 35, 44, 49 and 69 by courtesy of Leo Castelli Gallery and John Weber Gallery.

To my wife, Whee

In the recent developments of contemporary art, attempts have been made to find a coherent succession of styles such as the ones that marked the 1950's and the early 1960's. Anti-Form, Process Art, Arte Povera, Earth Art, Conceptual Art — these are some of the labels proposed during the last few years, but none is adequate to define the art of the late 1960's. Just as Pop Art and the Clement Greenberg school were becoming the established avantgarde, a whole new generation of artists appeared, engendering a situation much too broad and complex to be defined in terms of trends.

None of the artists presented in this essay can be associated validly with a particular school. Their works stem from original and personal views of what art ought to be. There are as many radically different views as there are artists in the book, and thus the dialogue between them is freed from controversies over forms and styles. Only a hidden net of subtle similarities in their approach to art and in their understanding of the contemporary situation allows me to present them together.

The lack of a dominant, strong unifying trend has inclined many observers to question the vitality of the late 1960's as compared to the immediately preceding period. When deprived of a frame of reference, it becomes difficult for the critic to acclaim the culture heroes, and the fluidity of the art scene may be misinterpreted as a sign of confusion or of decadence. The crowded parties of the days of Pop Art are gone and, to a certain extent, so are the big one-man New York retrospectives, the interest in the artist's social behavior, the direct influence of art on design and fashion, and the gamble of playing one style against another. These superficial changes in the art world reflect the contemporary artist's desire for more privacy and for more liberty in his artistic and intellectual life. If the term were not so overused, one could characterize the current scene as an " underground " situation. One of the possible reasons for the change lies in the end of the old Paris-New York feud, which resolved itself in an internationalism loosely centered in New York, but with intense peripheral activity in Germany, Italy, England, and even France. There is no more need for publicity and noise as it has become possible to approach the issues with an open-mindedness that favors the creative dialogue. Indeed, the artists who have appeared in the last five to seven years have shown an immense vitality, have presented many new alternatives, and have created extremely ambitious works.

Germano Celant in his book *Arte Povera,* Harald Szeeman in the exhibition " When Attitudes Become Form," and Kynaston McShine in his " Information " show, have defined this new international scene in a fairly convincing manner. Rather than rehashing their work and adding a few new names to the list, I have chosen to take the risk of being selective. My criterion has been the radicalism of a work rather than its quality, although in most cases the two concurred. From the different directions contemporary art has taken, I have chosen only one or two major artists, and I have limited my choice to those directions that deal with specific issues, defined later in the essay. Since I am concerned with the actual physical presence of the work in time and in space, I have eliminated both Lyrical Abstraction and Conceptual Art in its purest form.

✳

Criticism has long shown a tendency to enclose art in a system. Heinrich Wölfflin has done this brilliantly, and since his time almost every art historian has proposed a new system. The dialectic of thesis, antithesis, and synthesis still prevails, envisaging each new development as an evolutionary " answer " to the challenge of the preceding one. This is why, for instance, Anti-Form was considered a direct consequence of Minimal Art, which is the supreme affirmation of form. This is, however, only a very convenient short-sightedness, as the diversity — and, in this respect, the nonconformity — of the works proves. In order to understand how contemporary art emerged, it is necessary to forget about preconceived systems and to understand the characteristics of the general situation that was the platform for new creative departures in the mid-1960's. In other words, the question is not the usual "what could an artist do after a particular stage of stylistic development," but rather " what was an artist confronted with in his formative period." This involves art, culture, and society as well.

The 1960's were characterized by a deep identity and language crisis that troubled Western civilization. The definitions and the essential entities and values of life were questioned, negated, and replaced by new ones. A whole counter-culture based on music, political radicalism, drugs, and the writings of people such as H. Marshall McLuhan and Hebert Marcuse appeared. In the counter-culture that developed, oriental philosophies lost their exoticism and became widely vulgarized as a valid alternative to a Judeo-Christianism shaken by its blatant hypocrisies. Individual-centered philosophies became outdated and the intellectuals started to favor more analytical sciences such as anthropology, ethnology, or linguistics. The layman became much more aware of the consequences of the theory of relativity and of other discoveries concerning our thinking habits. But most important were the political and sociological traumas that placed the West in a position of deep self-doubt.

All the systems through which the individual has dealt with himself, with others, and with his environment, that is all the different forms of language, have come under critical examination. The traditional emphasis on the subject's action upon the object has been shifted in anthropology, ethnology, and linguistics, to the structure *between* the different objects. The subject in itself and the object in itself no longer constitute the main subject matter of sciences. This is even true in the realm of the more positivist sciences such as physics, in which the "uncertainty principle" marks the limit of the scientist's interest in the electron's exact nature and location in space. In all disciplines, the essence of things seems to be more than ever out of the human mind's reach. Philosophy and science are more preoccupied with systems and mechanism of functioning. In this intellectual revolution, the individual as subject or object has been wiped out, making Sartre's affirmation that "existentialism is humanism" correct, for it reflects an already-outdated belief in the individual's value. Much of the art of the late 1960's is directly connected with the above-sketched, new cultural orientations, despite what the comments of some of the leading thinkers of today might induce us to think. Let us for instance consider this argument by Claude Lévi-Strauss in *La Pensée Sauvage*: "Non-Figurative painting adopts manners and styles as its subjects; it claims to present a concrete representation of the formal conditions of all painting. The result is a paradox in that Non-Figurative painting does not, as it believes, create a work as real as — or more so than — the objects of the physical world, but realistic imitations of nonexistent models." One could not find better terms to express why a certain number of contemporary artists have completely rejected Abstract Art, not in order to go back to representation, but rather to experiment directly with the "physical world" in full acceptance of its inherent laws. Thus, Lévi-Strauss's critique is an extremely accurate one as long as it does not attempt to touch upon a form of art that essentially has nothing to do with Non-Figurative art. Here, the divorce between the artist and the philosopher is to be attributed to a lack of information and communication, just as in the case of Marcuse, who said in a lecture on the future of art given at the Guggenheim Museum that "[art] perpetuates that which *is* and prevents the realization of that which can and ought to be... [It does so] precisely inasmuch as it *is* form, because the artistic form (no matter how anti-art it strives to be) arrests that which is in motion, gives it limit and frame and place in the prevailing universe of experience and aspirations, gives it value in this universe, makes it an object among others." While this eventually sets the limits of the object in Conceptual Art (the written statements of the photographs), it does not apply to an art that openly acknowledges *time* within a work, and which is no longer concerned with the making of an "object." Here too, what seems to be a critique against contemporary art simply echoes the criticism against some aspects of art that appear in many of today's works.

✳

One of the strongest links between the artists presented here is an acute awareness of the weaknesses inherent in the accepted ideas about art. In 1967 Anti-Art celebrated its fiftieth anniversary; at this respectable age it could not continue as an intellectual game, but had to come to some kind of end. In the late 1960's there appeared to be three ways of dealing with an anti-art form of thinking. The first was to reject it entirely in favour of a return to what was most "artistic" in art, as the Lyrical Abstractionists did. Pushing it all the way toward purely intellectual analysis was another possibility chosen by the Conceptual artists, who deprived art of its physical existence. The way chosen by the artists presented in this book is yet another one. They retained a form of ethic derived from the different Anti-Art attempts, a mental habitat of rigorously questioning art through their work and of rejecting all the compromises with what art could no longer be. One of the main consequences of such an attitude is the refusal to place art on a pedestal and to judge it with "aesthetic indulgence." If art is to exist, it will only do so insofar as it is effective enough to find its place in real life. In most cases, this leads to a strengthening of not only the work's physical presence, but also its intellectual ratio. Not since Da Vinci have artists come so close in their creative-thinking process to the discoveries and conclusions of other realms of research such as physics, psychology, linguistics, and anthropology. Today's works have replaced vague, poetical allusion by a rigorous methodology in the experimenting with reality.

The mid-1960's can best be described as a platform with new possibilities and impossibilities originating from the works of the preceding generation. Ad Reinhardt, Jasper Johns, Robert Rauschenberg, Andy Warhol, and Frank Stella have not had, strictly speaking, any direct influence on the forms art has taken after them, but they did create a vast, challenging situation necessitating new alternatives.

One may question why I mention only painters, since I am dealing with three-dimensional art. An exception can be made for Mark Di Suvero who emphasized energy, structure, and materials in spatial situations. However, it is evident that during the 1950's and early 1960's sculpture raised fewer questions about the nature of art than did painting, whereas the contrary has become true since the mid-1960's. In this respect, the case of Ad Reinhardt is particularly illuminating. The analysis-purification of painting that he conducted through different styles in his entire work ultimately led him to his black-square paintings. These are kept from being perceived as objects through their minimal, bisymmetrical composition and their completely tuned-down colors. However, all the characteristics that were associated with "painting" — such as imagery, expression, composition, decorativeness, and chromatic qualities — have been eliminated from his work as nonessentials. Reinhardt has proved that a painting can most convincingly exist only as a painting and nothing else; in so doing he definitively closed this road for all artists concerned with a rigorous analysis of what painting essentially is. Nevertheless, Robert Ryman has managed, with his flat-white paintings, to disprove this assumption. In the 1950's there were only a few traces of a similar analytical-rejective form of thinking in sculpture (although it is noticeable in David Smith's "Cubi" series), and the potential for future three-dimensional art remained vast.

Traditionally, criticism has placed a barrier between the actual execution of the work and its ideal conception. All the arguments for or against "intellectualism" in art, for or against a clean, finished look, and even for or against subject matter originate from this need for categories. Such an attitude was challenged by Jackson Pollock's drippings, but it took the work of Jasper Johns to change radically "the critic's eyes." For him, thinking and creating are interconnected, and paint is a material applied with a tool as well as a medium for imagery. The painting can be and speak — even with wit, irony, or logic — and knowledge, memory, and perception coexist beyond critical classifications. Whereas Reinhardt analyzed art according to a "less is more" principle, Johns has shown how much more art actually can be. One extension of this all inclusive view of art is illustrated in Rauschenberg's preoccupation with the dichotomy between art and life in his combine-paintings. His point was so clear and decisive for the development of art that it does not need any further commentary. There is, however, a less important aspect of his work that should be emphasized in the light of the new art; he has demythicized technology, taking away the clean, rational, and basically optimistic undertone that it had naively adopted in the works of so many Kinetic artists. Technology is now merely an available medium for art, among all the other existing media; James Rosenquist made this clear as early as 1963 with his *Tumbleweed*.

As far removed as Warhol's work may be from what has been achieved in art after him, it is impossible to overlook him in trying to understand the works of the late 1960's. He was the first to integrate fully into his work as untreated facts the most diverse aspects of contemporary life, and to look bluntly at everything without giving a personal or moral judgment. He has shown an almost heroic ambition by completely disconnecting the artist's inner feelings from the finished work. After Warhol, such problems as "beautiful" or "ugly," "good," "bad," "optimistic," "pessimistic," and many others, have become old-fashioned to the point of somehow being distasteful and dishonest for an artist. Whatever one might propose after him would have to surmount the blasé, but forceful, "who cares" attitude underlying his entire work — a challenge that called for a new, convincing power in art.

Although Frank Stella's work has taken a different orientation in the past few years, his early black paintings and silver paintings decisively opened the door for the new ways of considering composition and space that occurred in the 1960's. He combined Reinhardt's lucidity with an inventiveness that allowed him to break through the boundaries of painting. Even his latest works, with their compositional complexities and their chromatic richness, are somehow much more than paintings — while still being paintings. This is because of the powerful way in which all of Stella's work reaches into actual space. By pulling the canvas away from the wall and by respecting the integrity of a simple compositional device in expansion, immediately graspable by the spectator, he created works that were neither truly paintings, nor sculptures, nor "objects," and which came very close to being what Donald Judd calls "specific objects."

The above-mentioned artists have created an unprecedented situation by somehow exhausting painting. Their works negate the possibility of offspring. It became evident after them that, whatever a painter would do, he would always be dealing with pictorial space, which by definition is not actual space. Artists now understood that they must come to grips with the only space that cannot be dismissed by the spectator — the real one. Painting has always been, and will always be, a tradition; for it can only be dealt with in terms of what the idea of painting is. To paint is to accept that art is abstracted from reality, and that it is a codified - no matter how vaguely - activity having its own particular space and time.

Sculpture is an entirely different matter. The term itself has no precise meaning. It merely covers the no-man's-land between painting and architecture, which is any kind of non-functional, three-dimensional artwork. However, for the average reader it suggests something that ranges from a "monument" to a "figurine." Whereas painting is definitely not reality, sculpture has the potential of being anything from a simple rock to a magic fetish. It encompasses all the different possible levels of abstraction from reality. The accepted idea of sculpture is one of a three-dimensional sign that is anthropomorphic, static, and self-centered. However, this is only what tradition has dictated. The artists I have chosen to discuss in this book have dismissed this limited idea of sculpture by allowing their work to become part of the real time-space continuum. Thus, they cannot be dealt with in terms of an aesthetic tradition, whether it be pictorial or sculptural, but rather, in terms of experience.

The main change brought about in the art of the late 1960's is a new conception of the nature of the artwork. Artists understood that it could no longer exist as an object abstracted from reality and merely dependent upon the different interplays and relationships between its elements. The work and the writing of Donald Judd offer the most convincing early example of a conscious attempt to break away from the artificiality of the work and give it a new status of existence. Mathematical series, actual physical conditions, and other obvious compositional devices were used to justify the form of a work of art. Thus, the internal relationships were either negated or rendered so evident, so immediately comprehensible, that the piece became extroverted. As Robert Morris pointed out in a letter to Jack Burnham, written on March 31, 1969, the problem was not to create " structure out of events, [but to use] structure much more consciously to build events." The events he is here referring to, it seems, are what happens between the spectator and the work and between space and the work. At this point, physicality becomes a main concern; for a piece can only be experienced validly if it is " no nonsense " and if it is present in actual space and time. It is interesting to remark that the shift from inside a work to its relationship with its surroundings corresponds to a new attitude toward the subject, typified by Mel Bochner's mention of the following statement by J. R. Weinberg: "Experience is simply whatever experimental facts there happen to be. It is quite impersonal and is not in any sense mine. In fact, except in the sense that 'I' am a certain configuration of experience, the word 'I' has no significance " (" Serial Art," *Arts Magazine*, Sum-

mer, 1967). Similarly, a work in itself has no more significance, except as a configuration of properties. This realization led artists to face problems such as the material's integrity, gravity, time, site, and dimension.

The art of the late 1960's marks the end of symbolism. A work exists by itself, not by its reliance upon a relationship with an aspect of reality somehow sublimated through the artistic process, or with the " ideal " of art to which Lévi-Strauss referred. This has been the most difficult change to accept and has brought about many misunderstandings. To say that Donald Judd and Carl Andre are still dealing with " the solidity, the tangibility of the ' recognizable ' formal vocabulary of Cubism and Constructivism " (Robert Pincus-Witten, " Fining it down," *Artforum*, June, 1970) is just as misleading as to relate Richard Serra's lead " splashings " to Pollock's drippings. In Max Kozloff's words, "... fairly obvious suggestions of prior art become mere manipulated ghosts of themselves in the tentative hassle with material itself." The radical departure from an idea of art as a symbolic system has been made by all the artists presented in this book, even those who have made a conscious use of symbols. Walter De Maria demonstrated it to those who had the chance of actually experiencing his pieces rather than simply seeing photographic reproductions of them. Thus, one of the oldest and most pervasive functions of Occidental art has been dropped and the way has been cleared for new definitions.

The purpose of this book is not to bring out the new definition of art, for this would only interest people who need categories between them and what they allegedly see. Rather, it is to leave the question open. It also intends to show the terms in which new alternatives are proposed in the works of artists who have dealt with the problems lucidly, without forgetting the primary importance of what is proposed to the eye and to the senses. Perception can never be dissociated from knowledge, from memory, and from the actual location in the time and the space of its occurrence.

Philosophical and critical writing has often attempted to define art, its value, its function, and its mode of being. Until the beginning of this century, very little of this theoretical questioning appeared in actual works of art. Kasimir Malevitch and the Dadaists were the first artists to challenge the accepted definitions of art, but the formal and stylistic implications of their works soon became more important than the more purely theoretical issues. Before the 1960's artists who chose to use three-dimensionality to find out what art ultimately is, indulged in exhibitionism and anticonformist rhetoric. In his questioning of paintings, Ad Reinhardt set the example of rigorous austerity. After him, it became necessary to extend this attitude to sculpture and to art in general.

During the 1960's, Dan Flavin, with his fluorescent-light sculptures, and Sol Lewitt, with his geometrical structures, approached the problem of art in a most straightforward manner. Their approach shares a common economy and effectiveness; for they demonstrate the possibility of actualizing pure theory in the perceived phenomenon through their work.

Carl Andre's is a parallel, but somehow different, approach. No less radical, he is more concerned with the sensorial qualities of material. For him theory does not exist before — or independently of — the time of the piece's existence. Of the three, he is also the one who focuses more specifically on sculpture and its inherent problem of verticality versus horizontality.

Flavin uses common objects, which exist momentarily as " pieces " once they are " plugged in. " They often modify the wall that supports them in the way a nonmaterial painting would. Sol Lewitt makes serial variations with a single geometrical volume, the cube, or with the basic elements of drawing. And Andre presents materials, grouping them according to a minimum of composition, such as simple addition or randomness. These visual propositions are in fact very different from each other, and each involves different problems. An obvious reason for grouping these artists together is their predilection for the use of straight lines and right angles. To allude to geometric art and once again to bring out the cliché of the " Cubist origin " would here be superficial and misleading.

None of these artists is interested in the straight line in itself: each merely happens to choose a so-called geometric vocabulary by necessity. The analytic approach that they share has forced them to reject all form that would be associative or evocative. A square, a rectangle, or a cube are nothing but a square, a rectangle, or a cube, existing in the specific situation created by the artist. They reveal something about art without confusing the work viewed with superfluous, secondary possibilities for interpretation. In some of their works, Sol Lewitt and Carl Andre have proven that elementary geometry or other equally neutral systems of composition, such as randomness, are equally valid means for their purpose. The analytical approach here referred to does not deal with forms, but with essence. What is? What is is? What is art? Can " being " be separated from " being here? " Is there an actual frontier between the artistic creation and its surrounding space, or is it only a mental category? These are abstract problems, but in the works of Flavin, Lewitt, and Andre, the spectator is physically confronted with them. This is the major difference between these artists and Conceptual artists such as Joseph Kosuth or Lawrence Weiner, who often deal with almost similar problems, but who do not feel the necessity of realizing their questionings in pieces, and thus voluntarily limit themselves to an *intellectual space.* Although Lewitt (who was in fact the first to use the term " conceptual ") particularly has been associated with Conceptual Art, his works are never immaterial. Mel Bochner has pointed out that " no thought can exist without sustaining support," which seems evident. This support, however, can be verbal, written, or physical. It is a traditional misconception to accept the two former supports as more adequate for conveying concepts. The three artists discussed in this chapter have clearly shown that an actual work, highly controlled, is a powerful generator of abstract ideas. By creating works that supersede the realm of artificial space (pictorial or intellectual), these artists have altered real space in such a way that the spectator literally bumps into pure ideas.

DAN FLAVIN

For those who believe that art should be about man, society, and life, art for art's sake is a gratuitous game whose only interest is decoration or intellectual entertainment. The combination of a title such as *Monument 4 for those who have been killed in ambush (to P. K. who reminded me about death)* with a sculpture made out of four fluorescent light tubes indicates that Flavin's position is more complex than just choosing between these two alternatives. The deep emotional charge of this title, as opposed to the cold simplicity of the work, is neither pretentiousness nor bad humor; the artist is conscious that both P. K. and those who have been killed in ambush are real. He himself has been familiar with death, first as a soldier in Korea in 1955, and later as an individual when he made an attempt, in 1959, at what he called "an irrelevant suicide." The true meaning of this title is an' ironical one, in the deepest sense of the word; it is a form of intellectual decency. It says just as much about what the piece is not as about what it is, making evident that there is only one way for an artwork to refer to something real with some decency and intellectual honesty; that is, not to refer to it at all. This became clear for Flavin in 1961. "I was tired," he wrote, "of my three year old romance with art mainly as tragic practice... I could begin again to change from so many small derived 'celebrations' to... much more intelligent and personal work."

After having explored Cézanne, Abstract Expressionism, and neo-Dadaist assemblages, Flavin made a clear break with traditional art. He started to juxtapose electric light bulbs with blank canvases in his first "Icons" (1962), which he has qualified as "dumb" if considered within the tradition of art as a codified system of forms.

A review of some other titles that he devised, gives a clue about what his art is and is not, indirectly speaking. Among the "Untitled" works, there are some dedicated "To Tatlin," "To Jasper Johns," "To Barnett Newman," "To Dorothy and Roy Lichtenstein," "To Donald Judd," and "To Sol Lewitt," among others. Are Flavin's pieces Constructivist? Is the fluorescent tube an "object?" Does the fluorescent light divide the space in the same way as a line, with a concentration of light-shadow, divides a canvas? Is Flavin concerned with the clean, industrial finish of a piece? Is he dealing with series and primary structures? Does a concept generate the form of the piece?

Flavin's pieces are about all these things, and about death too, in that he had to acknowledge it in order to create works that truly would no longer refer to it. There is not, indeed, any difference between the dedications that suggest an aesthetic problem and those that only refer to a personal relationship, such as "To Dick Bellamy," since both kinds deal with Flavin's life as an individual and not with the works themselves, which exist by themselves. The artist voluntarily abdicates from making any expression through the work. Personal feelings and aesthetic preferences remain in the background and do not interfere with what the piece is. According to Donald Judd, "things that exist exist. Everything is equal, just existing and the values and interest they have are only adventitious." Nothing, however, exists if there is nobody to say that it does. No value can be negated if it is not first acknowledged. Existence only means something inasmuch as one can grasp nonexistence. The fascinating power of Flavin's work lies in the tension between these extremes. It is not pushing logic to the absurd, but rather rigorously analyzing the nature of a phenomenon, getting down to its essence with an intellectual exigency and integrity that is also present in the work of Jacques Maritain, a neo-Thomist philosopher who interested Flavin during his formative years.

There is no place in this strict research for the old flirtation between art and handicraft. The fluorescent tubes are industrial products; they are put on the walls by electricians while the artist remains in the background. Flavin's role, however, is not merely to choose a ready-made object and to transform it into a work of art through his decision that it be one. His role is to place the tubes in a situation and to give them a function in space. What he creates is not so much an art object as it is the phenomenon of the piece's existence in a particular location, at a particular moment in time.

Most artworks are conceived as being independent from time, which deteriorates them, and from space, with which they interact. Flavin's pieces are, on the contrary, highly dependent. They *are* only when they are plugged in. They cease to exist when the fluorescent light is *dead*. They can *be* again when the tube is replaced. Within a certain period of time, all the parts of a piece could be replaced. Yet it would still be the same piece, which poses the question of what really "is" the piece. Because of their medium, Flavin's pieces cannot even be delimitated in space. The light takes on different qualities according to the quality of the natural light. The walls reflect the light, the fixtures create shadows on the walls, the colors react with each other, and the fluidity of the light negates the static quality of the fixture. This complexity raises one of the main questions inherent in his work: How do we relate to something, and through which intellectual categories do we do so?

Since he began using fluorescent lights, Flavin has completely stopped his artistic evolution. Essentially, all of his pieces are the same, dealing with the same basic problem. Flavin has, however, replaced the old idea of artistic evolution with another, more open, concept of free experimentation and inventory. In each piece, the fluorescent tubes are placed in a new situation that presents the problem from a different angle. In each case, the perceived phenomenon is a new one. Flavin's variations range from the single fluorescent tube placed diagonally on the wall (*The Diagonal of May 25*) to the most complex serial "compositions." Corner pieces, ceiling pieces, light tunnels, geometrical groupings, and barriers of light, these are some of the variations he has proposed. As he puts it, these are only "shifts on partitive emphasis modifying and addable without intrinsic change."

Einstein, in his generalized theory of relativity, used an image to show how dependent we are on a frame of reference in our relationship with reality. He imagined a physicist in an elevator that was moving very fast in intersidereal space. The physicist sees a bullet going through the walls of the elevator. Not knowing that he is in a moving elevator, he attributes to gravity the fact that the second bullet hole is lower than the first, whereas the real cause is the elevator's speed. Flavin proposes phenomena without frames of reference and most people become disoriented in their presence. If theater functions on the basis of a suspension of disbelief, Flavin's works require a difficult suspension of aesthetic beliefs from the spectator. They manifest the difficulty of facing a phenomenon without "framing" it. The enclosure of a room by *Untitled (To Dorothy and Roy Lichtenstein)* (1968-69) tends to remind the spectator of the artistic concept of environment. In other pieces, the use of colors such as blue, green, and pink allows subjective aesthetic preferences. The object itself, in an art context, is seen as an "icon."

Flavin can easily be misinterpreted if the critic introduces pictorial, architectural, sculptural, technological, environmental, and other concerns. But despite all that his pieces could be, they just simply *are*. This is their strength.

SOL LEWITT

It is a known fact that an actual "thing," whatever it is, never faithfully reflects its ideal concept. Since the time of Plato, philosophers have been concerned with the gap between the world of ideas and the world of reality. Sol Lewitt once said that "Conceptual artists are mystics." This is because their work involves a contemplation of the world of pure ideas. Lewitt's form of mysticism, however, is different from that of other Conceptual artists because his work situates itself in the unexplored area between the realms of ideas and of reality. This is an untenable and impossible situation; for the gap is irremediable. Thus, in a sense, all of Sol Lewitt's work is a failure. However, any pejorative meaning should be dismissed from this word because this is precisely his mystical dimension; for mystics concentrate all their energy toward the sublimation of their bodily condition, but still remain human beings. A mystic who could succeed would not be interesting at all. What is fascinating is the tension between the two extremes. Such a goal, in terms of art, is a very tough one because it involves the acceptance of whatever can happen once the concept, the "decision," has been chosen by the artist. The simpler the idea is, so too should be its materialization in a volume, but during this process of materialization it takes on unwanted

aesthetic qualities. Some of Lewitt's works are beautiful, some are boring, some are decorative, some are powerful, some are elegant; none, however, is a perfectly pure materialization of a concept, for the idea of materialization in itself implies impurity. Lewitt holds that a blind artist could perfectly well make art. This is true in respect to the conception of a work and even its realization, but this would be too easy an answer to the problem since the blind artist would not be responsible for all that could happen while the concept was being converted into form. The blind man would be better off, but the risk is denied him. Lewitt accepts the risk, and faces it consciously.

Lewitt's analysis touches upon one of the main problems of art: its essential duality as abstract *and* material. No work of art can escape this duality, but for a long time a work's materiality was deemed secondary (actually throughout all of "art history"), and a mere "suggestion" of the abstract realm was sufficient. Lewitt is not satisfied with such an essential ambiguity and has decided to explore it. In many senses his approach is parallel to the linguistic one, or to that of the French *Nouvelle Critique* as expressed by Roland Barthes: "A new depth has been added from now on to all the dimensions that delimitated and defined literary creation, the form constituting by itself a sort of parasitic mechanism of the intellectual function." What Lewitt attempts to do is to make evident, to analyze, and, finally, to control this parasitic mechanism of form.

This ideal of a controlled form manifests itself as an "order" that he gives to the person who will execute it. That the person might be Lewitt himself or somebody else does not matter as long as the integrity of the initial order is respected; that is, as long as no decision is taken in the course of the realization. Such an order can be, for instance, "build all the possible pairs by combining the following elements: one big square, one small square, one big cube, one small cube, the edges of one big cube, the edges of one small cube, one volume equal to two of the big cube, one volume equal to two of the small cube, the edges of one volume equal to two times the big cube, and the edges of one volume equal to two times the small cube." This is the ratio of his 1966 *Serial Project #1, sets A, B, C, D.* When actually realized, the work naturally becomes incredibly more complex than the initial "order." Lines and volumes interact; enclosing and enclosed are combined, as well as revealed and hidden; the dimensions take on another meaning according to their scale; the abstract notion of "edge" becomes a sculptural element; the faces of the cubes take on physical qualities; and the shadows change the piece as the observer moves around it.

Through his work, Lewitt has intuitively rediscovered the etymological meaning of the word "concept." In his early work, he was already concerned with containerlike volumes.

In them, he placed photographs inspired by those of Edward Muybridge, but only later did he discover that most of his "orders" — his concepts — when executed, were inevitably *enclosing* space just as a word encloses abstract qualities and takes an essence out of the nondefined, raw mental space. Making forms, in the final analysis, is like playing with those Russian dolls that contain each other, or like employing — as certain philosophic systems do — a system of the biggest common denominator in order to classify the real intellectually. Lewitt has experimented in the two opposite directions of enclosing something very big and of letting something small be enclosed. He once proposed to build a box around the Empire State Building, and also actually buried one of his small cubes.

The wall drawings that Lewitt has produced in the last two or three years reflect the same concern. In them as well, an abstract "order" is executed by somebody and involuntarily gets distorted. Even though his wall drawings are made directly on the walls, they very often take on "interesting" pictorial qualities and seem to relate to a kind of elegant geometric abstraction. In some recent ones, in which the initial "order" does not include the use of straight lines, the result even brings to mind the "soft labyrinths" encountered quite often in the drawings of schizophrenics. If this happens, however, it is neither Lewitt's fault, nor that of the person who "blindly" executes the drawing, but that of the order itself, for it cannot go from the realm of ideas to the realm of form without being distorted.

It is not the least amazing consideration that, when he passes from three to two dimensions, enclosing becomes "covering," just as an idea "covers" a certain aspect of reality, all of which suggests that Sol Lewitt has succeeded in eliciting the nature of the inevitable gap between the world of ideas and the world of objects.

CARL ANDRE

"In the days of form, people were interested in the Statue of Liberty."
"Now sculptors aren't interested in Eiffel's structure anymore."

CARL ANDRE (interviewed by PHYLLIS TUCHMAN, *Artforum*, June, 1970).

Carl Andre is specifically concerned with sculpture and with the activity and role of the sculptor. Before approaching his work, some considerations about the accepted definitions of sculpture are necessary. Admittedly, this art is the making of a three-dimensional sign. It transforms matter into something that can express the message of the artist in a spatial situation. This is the accepted definition, which every sculptor has taken for granted up to now, but which has never been analyzed further.

Linguistics, since the time of Ferdinand de Saussure, have established a major distinction within the sign: on one hand there is meaning; on the other, that which carries the meaning (for example, in the word "tree," the actual sound "tree" *or* the actual form of the written word). This distinction between the signified and the signifier helps us to comprehend better the nature of any language, including sculpture, which is a whole formed out of two elements, each of which can be examined independently. When art criticism deals with the work of an artist, it inevitably tends to emphasize the signified and to forget about the signifier. Even formalist criticism, with its more objective approach, fails in its dealing with the signifier as such, separated from the meaning it can take. This is because criticism speaks from the observer's point of view rather than from that of the maker. From this standpoint, the search for a definition of the signified is the search for a valid "justification" of the piece's presence or existence. On one hand, there is matter and the handling of matter; on the other hand, are the balance, the tensions, the harmony, and the evocation of such things as ideas and sentiments, which artists put into matter. To emphasize the second aspect might be a complete misunderstanding of what sculpture primarily is.

The idea that a sculptor is a man who wants to express something and who uses material to do so is another traditional concept that has never been questioned. What if he simply confronts matter and experiences the need to deal with it, in much the same way as any living creature with vocal cords feels the need to exercise them, no matter how articulate or inarticulate the sounds he produces might be? If this be the case, the problem of meaning is transposed to another level. Going back to linguistics, to understand the sound "tree" is to understand no longer that it means "tree" but to see how such a sound reveals the relationship of a certain society to reality, as opposed to those of societies who use the words "Baum" or "arbre." In terms of art criticism, this implies the abandonment of the search for a meaning in order to justify a piece, and the start of tackling the complexities involved in handling matter itself.

The first time one feels the necessity of physically dealing with the material world is in early childhood. A child has three basic ways of doing this. One is to deform, reform, mutilate, or shape; that is, to change the form of a given material into a new form. Another is to combine, put together, glue, nail, pile, or, in other words, to create a unifying structure between heterogeneous materials. The last possibility is simply to take the material and, in order to differentiate it from other materials, give it a personal value. Often, the most nondescript piece of wood, plastic, or rubber is treasured by a child, who has imbued it with special properties. Throughout all of our relationships with the material world, these three basic attitudes can be observed. Sculpture and architecture, in particular, tend to have different styles according to the particular attitude of the creator. The work of Le Corbusier and Hans Arp, as well as African huts or Minimal Art exemplify the concern for form; Constructivism, Anthony Caro, Gothic architecture, or contemporary urbanism are in search of the unifying structure; and Marcel Duchamp is the perfect artistic manifestation of the third attitude.

The split between sculpture and architecture occurs when the notion of function is introduced; for, in the case of architecture, function orients the spontaneous impulse toward something directly and immediately useful to society. At this point, sculpture is left disoriented, without apparent purpose. This fact gives rise to the introduction of meaning and the emphasis upon the signified in order to justify sculpture in the viewer's eyes.

Carl Andre has summarized his artistic evolution, from his early wood sculpture in the manner of Constantin Brancusi, to his pilings of simple wood elements, to his floor pieces, by saying that he has gone from form to structure to place. Nonetheless, this statement is only an approximation, for his latest pieces have a definite form and structure. What Andre has done is to systematically avoid all that justifies sculpture. In order to do so, he was forced to reject all forms that could be construed as being representational or signifying. Later, he had to do the same for structures. What he has done, according to linguistics, is to attempt to separate the signifier from the signified. "To say," explained Andre, "that art has a meaning is mistaken because then you believe that there is somo message that the art is carrying like the telegraph, as Noël Coward says" (Carl Andre, interviewed by Phyllis Tuchman, *Artforum*, June 1970). Andre's concept of place, then, takes on a more subtle meaning in that the sculpture is not an environment, an architecture, or a geographical location, but the place where the dealing with the material occurs, both for the spectator and for the artist himself.

The emphasis on place implies, as we have seen, that the material *is* the place, but it also implies that it is *in* a place. The relationship between the material and the location creates a new possibility for meaning unless it is controlled by the artist. For instance, platinum in an outdoor, muddy space would carry just as much sign-value as any form or structure. Indeed, Andre must avoid any kind of tension in this relationship in order to preserve the integrity of his works. In most instances, the chosen material is naturally integrated with the environment. Bricks and metal plates blend with the architectural spaces, haystacks are placed on the edge of a forest, a pile of rocks in the mountains, or raw wood beams on earth. The strength of these pieces is in the "minimal," but real and effective, transposition of a chosen space.

Andre's treatment of structural problems reveals these very same preoccupations. He seems to realize that there is no way of avoiding a horizontal composition; in his early Brancusian works, the vertical ascent is a step-by-step succession of horizontals added to each other. Horizontality is what we know — is what is here; if sculpture rises in space, it runs the risk of becoming just an artificial construction whose very structure takes on more importance — as a sign — than the fact of the sculpture itself. Horizontality, therefore, is almost an ethical limitation, as is the threat of aphasia, ever present in the writing of Samuel Beckett. There are aspects of Andre's work that bring him close to some existentialist concerns, especially if one compares his emphasis on the signifier versus the signified within the work of art with Sartre's emphasis on existence versus essence within the individual's life.

Another of Andre's compositional devices is his use of anaxial symmetry, "a kind of symmetry in which any one part can replace any other part" (ibid.). In terms of signification, this is a kind of nonstructure, also encountered in the pure random distribution of particles ("the symmetry of the heavens," ibid.), which he has often used in his work.

Going from structure to the actual form of the different elements in Andre's pieces, one can find similar concerns. The square shape he has chosen for most of his works has almost no interest as a sign. Its only connotation would be the psychological undertone of the concept "square" (not tricky, frank, clear) and a lack of dynamic orientation, whereas the shape of works, like *Aluminum Ribbon Piece*, is casually fortuitous, determined not by the artist but by the material itself as it falls on the floor.

Andre has managed to delete from sculpture all that can distract one's attention from the dealing with material, by means of an intellectual as well as an intuitive approach. As a flyer for one of his exhibitions, he used Mendelyeev's table of elements, which was a way of presenting a simplified structure and also of making a very didactic statement about the primary importance of materials. His works, however, do not exemplify a theory; they propose a real experience to the spectator. Although visual, this experience encompasses almost all the other senses; for, what Andre proposes is a ground contact to be perceived through one's feet, eyes, and sense of density as well as through the sounds one hears when walking upon the piece. His works provide the possibility of having a new relationship with reality, freed from all the alienating "meanings" that separate us from it.

Nothing in Carl Andre's works is abstracted. Because he has refused to give art a special status of existence, he has accepted all the occurrences that might alter the piece; for scratches, traces of human contacts, rust, and other marks of time are all recorded on the piece.

II

In *The Aims and Methods of Scholarship in Modern Language and Literature,* Northrop Frye suggests that "the primary understanding of any work of literature has to be based on an assumption of its unity. When we reach the end of a poem or of a novel," he continues, "we can see the whole design of the work as a unity. It is now a simultaneous pattern radiating from a center, not a narrative moving in time." Considered as a whole, the various works of an artist are in many ways similar to a literary work. The creations follow each other in a succession similar to narrative time, and each has its particular characteristics. But in the final analysis, the creations are all related to a central point that escapes narrative time and which invests them with their shape and structure. To a large extent, art is always about art, and so is art criticism. What differentiates them is their position in relationship to this "central point." For the artist, inasmuch as this point is his, it is unique; for the critic, there are as many "central points" as he can find in the different works he studies, which, in a sense, makes him freer than the artist. No matter how far from his work the artist wishes to be, he will always be the central locus from which a unifying structure emanates, and he is unable to do anything to contradict it. Psychology explains this by the concept of identity that the artist transmits into the work, and which has been one of the main bases of Occidental art.

Marcel Duchamp, nevertheless, proved that art without identity is possible. For fifty years, there has not appeared a single critical analysis of his work that has succeeded in pinpointing its basic orientation, simply because there is no basic orientation other than the refusal to have an orientation. Duchamp is an alchemist. Duchamp is an optical artist. Duchamp is a Futurist. Duchamp is a chess player. Duchamp is a Dadaist. Duchamp is an erotic poet. Duchamp is able to be all of these things because his attack on tradition was an essential one. He made the identity explode. By depriving his work of a central point, he brought it very close to art criticism, and instead of reviewing existing possibilities, he negated everything and opened the way for new directions in art.

It is interesting to note that in their writing both Morris and Smithson have covered with great lucidity all the major issues of sculpture. Unlike artists such as Vassili Kandinsky, who exposed one unified aesthetic theory in his writing, they have both shown an awareness of the diversity, the complexity, and the contradictions in the debating of ideas. But the very openness that contributes to the quality of their writing is difficult for some people to accept when it appears in their work. For many people are still conditioned by the old tradition of art based upon the "sacred" attachment to the concept of identity, which is questioned by these two artists.

Smithson's interest in the process of sedimentation gives a clue to his attitude toward this problem. Sedimentation never ceases. It is a process that is concurrent with time. It keeps adding new to the old without preconceived order, and constantly changes the identity of the whole. His art is, indeed, a form of sedimentation of life — not of his own life, but of all that he knows to be existent, and this includes geology, science fiction, film, literature, history, sociology, architecture, and all the major developments of contemporary art. Morris's approach is somehow more restrictive, but just as difficult to grasp. As Jack Burnham wrote in the March, 1970 issue of *Artforum,* "Morris's sculpture is essentially criticism about sculpture... With him, the aesthetic of 'the found object' has been exchanged for the found art movement... It will be some time before all the implications of such aesthetic decision-making are clear to us."

ROBERT MORRIS

Two early works by Robert Morris reveal his anticonventional treatment of the problem of identity within a work of art. The first, made in 1961, is *Box with the Sound of its Own Making.* The other, dating from 1963, is an "Untitled" box with a door, which opens on a photograph of a box with a door, itself open. In both of these works, there is an unstable ontological situation comparable to that of man himself who is able, as a subject, to see his "self" as an object. Psychoanalysis shows that, in extreme cases, the "self" as a subject dissociates itself entirely from the "self" as an object, just as an observer is separated from the object of his observation. Unlike any sculpture that exists as a unified whole in space and in time, these two works are able to see and hear themselves, even before being fully materialized as pieces. Thus, they must be something else than what they appear to be; they *are* in a different time and space dimension. The varieties of forms that Morris's art has taken during the past decade, either invented, or inspired by the works of artists such as Johns, Judd, Serra, or Nauman, are many masks of what his art really is. The problem of influences is no longer relevant. Paradoxically, what is of main importance for Morris is not so much the form of the piece, but the knowledge of the spectator. The work is no longer in Morris's words " an irreversible process ending in a static icon-object," but the uncovering of what happens between the spectator and a physical reality. The work is different for each spectator according to what he knows about the structure of the entire physical reality. As a whole, Morris's work is a kind of casual maieutic whose effectiveness stems out of his awareness of the rules of spatio-temporal sensorial perception, and of his understanding of history. Morris is an artist who makes art as well as one who sees and judges art. His work reveals his unusual ability to remove himself completely from what he is doing in order to tackle another problem. He is continually stepping over the boundary separating the outsider, such as the critic or general public, and the artist, and thus becomes detached enough to think mainly in terms of art history.

It is possible to see all of Morris's pieces as examples of almost all the major issues raised by the three-dimensional art of the mid-1960's. The L-shaped beams of 1964 will remain some of the clearest statements about the issues raised by Minimal Art. With their flat gray-white color, they resist any attempt to find an interest within themselves. They are, as Morris suggests in " Notes on Sculpture — Part 2 " (*Artforum*, October, 1966), " but one of the terms " of the aesthetic experience. The space that surrounds them, the light, the spectator's motion around them, as well as other external factors become more important than what happens inside them. Although there is an immediately graspable Gestalt, the work really requires additional time to be completely experienced, since it depends upon all the external variables that interact with its psychological idea (the L-shaped volume). When the different details of a surface or the relationships between complex volumes catch the spectator's eye within a sculpture, within its " intimacy," the piece starts to live in its own completely abstracted time. Inevitably, it becomes a sort of " story " that has its limits in terms of real time. With Minimal Art, on the contrary, " the known constant and the experienced variable " (ibid.) constantly interplay in a real time continuity. Another point clearly demonstrated by these L-shaped pieces is that " placement becomes critical as it never was before in establishing the particular quality of the work " (ibid.). Using the same volume, Morris has created a set of nine completely different works by placing the *L* in nine different positions, while it really is the same piece. This then raises the crucial problem of perception. In the realm of ideas, what is, is; the artist conceives a certain specific volume that is nothing other than what it is. The spectator is able, according to the Gestalt theory, to abstract all the details or variables in his act of perception in order intellectually to grasp what was conceived by the artist. However, the total experience of perception tells us that, in the case of these pieces, *how* we perceive them becomes more important than *what* they are. In other words, Morris shows us that the Gestalt is only part of the experience of perception, in which our own mental training to relate to the world in terms of verticality, horizontality, directions, masses, distances, and light intensity, becomes the main determining factor. What we see is not an L-shaped beam, but just something that reacts with these categories, something that is positioned in a particular space, and which has a dimensional relationship with the size of the human body.

Morris deals with issues and isolates them in his pieces in a unique manner. Compared to him, the other Minimal sculptors seem to be making art and are less concerned with clearly-formulated aesthetic problems. He, on the other hand, is giving a powerful, didactic demonstration of what sculpture is.

The relationship between the space inside the piece and the space outside it is another issue that Morris has dealt with in numerous sculptures. *Untitled* (1968), *Aluminum I-Beams*, is a slanted square of 180″ x 180″ formed by four heavy beams and elevated on one side at 54″ from the ground. In this work there is a constant interplay between the perception of the actual material, the perception of the slanted plane and the perception of a volume delimited by the beams. This is another way of demonstrating the mechanism of perception, in that a raw physical fact cannot be perceived without getting processed in the mind according to a Euclidean conception of space.

There is little doubt that it is this acknowledgment of a processing of the visual data into intellectual categories that prompted Morris to try to make it more difficult. Without this processing stage of perception, the contact with the piece itself would become even more direct. Morris is aware that " an order, any order, is operating beyond the physical things " (" Beyond Objects, Notes on Sculpture — Part 4, " *Artforum*) and thus is actually separating us from the physical things. His Anti-Form attitude is in fact an anti-order attitude, or, at least, an anti-*imposed* order. Whatever is presented, there is always an order, but the problem is to know if the artist has artificially imposed this order on the material according to an intellectual logic, or if it is the order of the material itself, obeying only natural laws. His " felt pieces " of 1968-69 serve as a good answer to this problem. Hanging from the wall as they do, they naturally take the form imposed by gravity upon their specific physical characteristics. They have no fixed, definitive form, but change according to the differences in the physical condition of each new situation. For the spectator, the only *graspable* thing in terms of Gestalt is the remnant of the action that the artist has performed upon the material: processes such as cutting, piling, or hanging set the limits of the material's freedom and allow the understanding of a certain range of possible forms.

The very fact of being able to focus on a work of art is sometimes enough to take it out of reality and to transform it into an artistic "something else." The nature of perception is such that focusing produces images or even icons. Morris was aware of this fact long before he made his 1968 mixed-media pieces, which fill the whole available space with elements of equal interest, and which thus make it impossible to focus and impose the piece upon the spectator's whole angle of vision. In an early dance piece, *21.3*, he quoted *Studies in Iconology* by Erwin Panofsky: "... what I see from a formal point of view is nothing but the change of certain details within a configuration that forms part of the general pattern of color, lines and volumes which constitute my world of vision. When I identify, as I automatically do, this as an event (the removing of a hat for instance), I have already overstepped the limits of purely formal perception and entered a first sphere of subject matter or meaning..." By creating rooms in which there is nothing worth identifying, Morris has placed the spectator in a vulnerable position, verifying the fact that, in everyday life, " the sphere of meaning " acts as a bumper between man and reality.

Whereas Morris's theories on art have evolved step by step and are exemplified by very didactic pieces, the rest of his œuvre jumps from one problem to another, occasionally going back to re-examine an abandoned issue. It often seems as if his works were clearly divided between those in which he explores a new problem and those in which he develops what he already knows. His 1970 exhibition at the Whitney Museum included good examples of the second category. The anti-order attitude that originated with the " felt pieces " took on an impressive dimension in his two large Whitney Museum pieces; namely, a toppled stack of timber and a complex work composed of a double wooden track on which hollow blocks of concrete were pushed over with the help of steel rollers until they fell between the broken tracks. In the second piece especially, which measured some ninety-five feet, there was an almost theatrical effect of chaos. It was created by the antagonism between man-imposed order and the disorder, or natural order, of the final configuration of the piece, which was essentially the result of the artist's disordering action and the forces of gravity.

Morris's most recent theoretical explorations deal with the pure analysis of the mechanisms of perception, without the support of a real piece of sculpture. Among the other problems he touched upon is that of the relationship between memory and perception, which was already underlying the Minimal sculptures. In a work shown at Finch College, New York, Morris filmed the four walls of a room and projected the film, with a rotating projector, upon these same walls, creating an overlap between image and reality, between the image's time and real time, a feat that echoes the overlap between the memory of a thing and the perception of the same thing. At the Guggenheim's VIth International, he used a video camera and a television screen to construct an even more didactic piece in which it was possible to watch what had happened a few seconds earlier in real life on the screen. Both of these pieces seem to refer to the 1963 box discussed above and indicate that beyond Morris's handling of materials and objects, there is a highly controlled handling of the spectator's mind.

ROBERT SMITHSON

Art has long shared the assumption with theater that, in order to be fully appreciated, exterior conditions must be forgotten. It has been said that one of the criteria for judging a play is the ability to forget how hard the chair is. Sculpture, in particular, always, required much oblivion; the spectator had to forget about its location, its literary connotations, its formal relationships with other objects, and about the technical problems of its making. There is a psychological reason for this. For him who is making a piece of art, the world is divided between what is the piece and what is not the piece. The former is under control and intentional; the latter, out of reach and out of control. The artist creates a particular kind of relationship with his work, a highly exclusive one that tends to take the work completely out of reality. Because of this, artists are generally reluctant to have their art judged in any other terms than purely aesthetic ones. This tendency has been reflected in most critical writing, especially in that by Clement Greenberg. There is a deep contradiction between contemporary art's attempt at reaching a convincing degree of reality and this kind of *special* attitude taken when making or facing a work of art. It is often difficult for the person who is not entirely in the work, but simply in the world, to accept the limitations required by such an attitude.

Robert Smithson has been able to take enough perspective from his work to be able to handle all these aspects that we customarily consider " secondary " in the artistic experience. His dialectic between site and nonsite is an emphasis upon the problems involved in the two alternatives of either leaving the work in reality or of taking it out of its context to place it in a new one. It implies the acceptance of the conditions specific to each context, and also forces the spectator to acknowledge what is not the work of art.

Smithson's evolution goes from Minimal to Earth Art with consistency. He has understood all the major issues of this development of sculpture and has created works that reflect his understanding. But this is not really the point, since art is not a closed system for him. Rather than examining his artistic evolution and analyzing it in terms of aesthetics and art history, I have chosen one of his recent works, *Spiral Jetty*, in order to show how it remains open to many interpretations.

Smithson made a film of this piece, which gives some of the directions from which one might derive an interpretation. It includes views of the earth, of the machinery, of the lake, of the crystals formed where water meets earth, of dinosaurs in the New York Museum of Natural History, of the solar eruptions, of the maps of the location, and of the film's editing room. There is very little indeed about art history references. Nevertheless, most of the directions proposed by this film come very close to specific issues that are important for contemporary sculpture.

The very form of the work, a spiral, is an open one, which, in terms of Gestalt, is impossible to grasp without accepting the notion of the infinite. Contrary to all the Minimal artists who have been preoccupied with cubic volumes, which have a "closed" Gestalt, Smithson has always preferred volumes that imply a geometric progression. Thus, he has originated a dynamic Gestalt; for the perception of the piece implies more than the three spatial dimensional axes, it implies the understanding of a development in time. Smithson's allusion to the sun and to the dinosaurs is a way of reminding us of the special dimensions of the spiral, and its geometric configuration is a symbol of evolution. Furthermore, next to the hall of the Museum of Natural History that contains the dinosaurs, there is a large spiral on a wall, tracing the evolution of life on earth.

Another important aspect of Smithson's movie is its insistence on the actual location of the work, not only through the shots of maps and through the panoramic views of the site, but also through the symbolism of the long road that one must follow in order to reach the site. Smithson is not the only artist to have noted that contemporary sculpture cannot be dissociated from its place of location. But, whereas this relationship of the work to its location is generally an almost abstract one based upon space, dimensions, and physical properties, with him it is an all-inclusive one. The site, with all its aspects, is both the work and its context.

Describing one of his *Mirror Displacements,* Smithson writes: "The road went through butterfly swarms. Near Bolonchen de Rejon thousands of yellow, white and black swallowtail butterflies flew past the car in erratic, jerky flight patterns. Several smashed into the car radio aerial and were suspended on it because of the wind pressure. In the side of a heap of crushed limestone the twelve mirrors were cantilevered in the midst of large clusters of butterflies that had landed on the limestone. For brief moments flying butterflies were reflected; they seemed to fly through a sky of gravel. Shadows cast by the mirrors contrasted with those seconds of color. A scale in terms of time rather than space took place. The mirror itself is not subject to duration, because it is an ongoing abstraction that is always available and timeless. The reflections, on the other hand, are fleeting instances that evade measure. Space is the remains, or corpse, of time, it has dimensions. Objects are sham space, the excrement of thought and language. Once you start seeing objects in a positive or negative way you are on the road to derangement. Objects are phantoms of the mind, as false as angels. Itzpaplotl is the Mayan Obsidian Butterfly..." (*Artforum*, September, 1969). In this case, a work made in a specific location, namely Yucatan, not only acknowledges the particular characteristics of soil and of the space, but also of the flora, the fauna, and the legends linked with the site. All these elements concur to give the work different layers of meaning, all intimately interrelated in the "real situation," and referring to the stratified continuity of experiences outside the work.

In the case of *Spiral Jetty*, Great Salt Lake was chosen because of its physical properties, notably a high density of a salt that gives it a reddish color and which crystallizes on the lake's border and on the work itself. But *Spiral Jetty* acquired an additional meaning when Smithson discovered old legends claming that the lake is connected with the ocean, and telling of a dangerous whirlpool, of which the *Spiral Jetty* becomes a magical symbol. Mentions of *Loveladies, Atlantis,* and the *City of Snakes*, are other examples of Smithson's interest in history and legends; as is the following quote: "Coatlicue said: You have no future, and Chronos said: you have no past... but Coatlicue concludes: You don't have to have existence to exist" (ibid.). Unreality is part of the work's reality. There is no limit between the past, the present, and the future. Categories are shaken and start to crumble, exposing deeper structures of understanding.

The construction of an art object implies a certain number of limiting choices. Geometrical or anthropomorphic manmade forms are but limited sets of forms. They create boundaries in terms of quality by being distinct from natural forms. Smithson's handling of material, such as trucks pouring earth and rocks into the lake, allows for formal diversity and complexity. Such a methodology is suitable for him because it terminates in a more physical result and because it escapes the fatality of artificial formal boundaries: the spiral and the lake exist on the same level of reality. Thus, Earth Art is an aesthetic choice as well as a door open on the "oceanic." It is the materialization of Smithson's wish to constantly risk an art that stays in Ehrenzweig's dedifferentiation field, encompassing in the same space and time the particular and the universal, the past and the future, and all that is antithetic only in our tradition of "differentiated" thinking.

As Smithson himself stated, such an attitude challenges the critic's sense of limits and his reluctance to suspend the boundaries between "self" and "nonself."

III

"We experience more than we can analyse."
A.N. WHITEHEAD
*"Sensibility is inclusive and precedes analytic aware-
ness."* ANONYMOUS

Quoted by RICHARD SERRA, *Arts Magazine,* February, 1970.

In the 1960's sculpture moved away from a self-centered intimism and began to reach into real space. The spectator was offered the possibility of relating to it in terms of real experience rather than in terms of aesthetic contemplation. Correlative to this change was the disappearance of boundaries between purely visual and other forms of perception. The artist no longer created an " art object," but could set up the physical conditions of a complex phenomenon. There was a new independence of the piece from the categories formed by divisions between the different senses. The piece was like a raw fact, in itself no more visual than auditive, tactile, olfactory, or even mnemonic or intellectual. This was already implicit in Carl Andre's pieces, inasmuch as their perception includes the sound they make when walked upon and a feeling of the density of the various materials. The work of art, autonomous from man, radiates all sorts of energies due to its physical properties. At the moment of perception, these energies become stimuli, channeled through the senses. The best works of Richard Serra, Keith Sonnier, or Bruce Nauman seek to disrupt or disturb the usual patterns of the channeling or of the coding of sensorial stimuli.

Traditionally, studies in human communications have designated the word as the main element of communication, the real " meaning-carrier," and intonation and behavior have been considered mere frames. Recent developments in kinesics — the science of body motion — have shown that this is an inadequate, if not completely false, conception. Speech and behavior are now recognized as a complex continuum whose different elements constantly interact. Only the observer's inability to properly codify this multileveled system has compelled him to isolate the single element of speech. In much the same way, the difficulty of dealing with a complex sensorial system has inclined artists and critics to isolate and focus exclusively upon the purely visual aspect of art, while relegating almost every other aspect (except the intellectual, which is codified in terms of literature) to the province of unimportant contingencies.

Serra, Sonnier, and Nauman share the same concern for enlarging and making more complex the perceptual experience. Before them, Happenings, performances, and environments such as Whitman's, attempted to deal with similar problems, but a so-called Pop sensibility pervaded these experiments; that is, they were not disturbed by a theatricality that can arise from the use of images and icons. We are now clearly in a post-Minimal sensibility. These three artists are aware that a work no longer refers to anything other than itself, and that it no longer necessitates an accommodation to special, non-natural, spatio-temporal conditions. All three artists must serve a tight balance, tending toward rendering perception more complex, yet respecting the limitations that prevent them from lapsing into " artificiality." Technology has been quick to adopt a sociological undertone in modern art. This has caused the failure of many technological environments and other amateurish displays of hardware that have appeared in galleries and museums. Nauman's videotapes and " corridors " and Sonnier's most recent works, as well as Serra's use of films, have proved that technology offers a large, new repertory of media to the artist who knows how to de-emphasize its technological aspects. What is here proposed is a new, very cool, but highly sophisticated exploitation of everything that science has made available. In comparison with what the relationships between art and technology have been, this attitude is truly revolutionary.

Multisensorial perception, as conceived by Serra, Sonnier, and Nauman, opens the way for a new approach to spatial problems. The study of animal behavior shows that it is possible to deal with space with great precision and control in terms other than those of geometry. For an animal's instinctive mapping out of his territory is not three-dimensional, but is synthetic of all his experiences within this territory. In other words, the animal's conception of space consists in a mapping of sensorial stimuli, while our own consists in a volumetric abstraction. When artists spoke about spatial problems in sculpture, it was in terms of " full " versus " empty." The sentiment of danger and weight emanating from Serra's " lead props," the areas of high-density light or of high-density sound in Sonnier's works, and the front-back reversal that happens in some of Nauman's " corridors " clearly relate to a nonabstract treatment of space. They create conditions that force the spectator to rediscover his own instinctive relationships with a multidimensional space without relying upon three-dimensional geometry.

RICHARD SERRA

"The spectator not only sees the represented elements of the finished work, but also experiences the dynamic process of the emergence and assembly of the image just as it was experienced by the author. And this is, obviously, the highest possible degree of approximation to transmitting visually the author's perception and intention in all their fullness, to transmitting them with that strength of physical palpability with which they arose before the author in his creative work and his creative vision: 'Not only the result, but the road to it also, is a part of truth. The investigation of truth must itself be true, true investigation is unfolded truth, the disjuncted members of which unite in the result.'"

S. M. Eisenstein, *The Film Sense.*

In analyzing Richard Serra's work, it is impossible to dissociate the physical properties of a piece and the psychological conditions of its perception. Materials, processes, thought mechanisms, time, horizontality, verticality, composition, weight, disorder, perspectives, Gestalt, Knowledge, structures, and physicality are some of the different aspects under which his pieces may be considered, but they are actually all interconnected. They form a complex system whose functioning is uncovered by Serra when he emphasizes a few of these aspects in unexpected orders. His pieces, however, are not "demonstrations" in the cold and rational sense of the word, for they have none of the abstract and timeless qualities of an aesthetic theorem. Rather, they place the spectator in conditions that force him to participate almost physically with their inert action.

Serra's "Prop" pieces, in which several tons of lead are in precarious balance, bring into focus sculptural, conceptual, and other issues, but never make statements about these issues. It is through the experience of their sheer weight and potential for collapse that one understands the point, which thus becomes crucial to the very existence of the piece, rather than abstract and theoretical. The "Prop" pieces show the actual struggle of sculpture trying to rise in space without having recourse to artificial building devices such as "points, clips, gluing, welding," which are "unnecessary and irrelevant" (Richard Serra, *Arts Magazine*, February, 1970). This is a way of accepting Andre's challenge of truth to materials without accepting its limiting consequences. In his "Prop" pieces, Serra avoids horizontality by using gravity rather than by artificially building *against gravity* as does traditional sculpture. The *Skullcracker Series* of 1969, which are pieces thirty feet high, constructed with stacked chunks of steel ("crop, the

waste product of the hot mill"), defy gravity in the simple process of piling, by a system of hazardous weight and counterweight, until they reach a point at which they "both tend upward and collapse downward toward the ground simultane-ously" (ibid.) But in the "Prop" pieces, the handling of gravity is carefully calculated and does not depend on chance. The weight of some elements is aimed at counterbalancing the weight of the others, so that the different forces tend to negate each other and to reach stabilization. Each element, with its particular positioning, is a necessary one. The slightest change in the structure would be enough for it to collapse. "Nothing gratuitous" is not only an aesthetic ideal, it is the sine qua non condition of the work's existence. Of these pieces Serra wrote that "the perception of the work in its state of suspended animation, arrested motion, does not give one calculable truth like geometry, but a sense of presence, an isolated time" (ibid.). This feeling of presence is not caused by the aesthetically related forms and volumes of mere constructivist sculpture; there is a head-on confrontation with the real tensions of the forces, the fragility of this state of order reached for a period of time by the piece, and the zone of real danger which surrounds it.

How a piece was built, which physical laws are structurally employed, what are the intrinsic properties of its material — an instinctive understanding of these questions is part of the work's perception. Serra not only deals with forms, but also with our knowledge of the physical world. In so doing, he extends Minimal Art's concern with Gestalt beyond the perception of pure form into a more complex realm of multilevel perception. But the principle of simplicity and avoidance of details is respected on each of these levels. Serra's use of gravity is, in this respect, as simple as Minimal Art's use of cubic volumes; it has the same effectiveness. The complexity only emerges when the different levels interact. Rather than follow the patterns that we instinctively recognize as normal or accepted, Serra redistributes the elements. His films generally treat one simple, elementary subject, such as the measuring of a frame, but his very discourse challenges the spectator's need for ready-made solutions and certitudes in a manner that is sometimes similar to that of Michael Snow. Very often, the result is attained by using the camera both as a device for filming and as an object whose specific qualities and functions are recorded on the film. The perception of what is being filmed and the perception of the film being made create two levels of perception between which there is a constant interplay.

In his films as well as his sculptures, Serra manages to be "conceptual" by emphasizing the physical aspect of the work. The material is there. It is not abstracted because it is its own information, and it does not apport information about something else as is otherwise the case in art. These pieces are not icons, symbols, or signs; they are self-explanatory. This refers to what has been pointed out about signifier and signified in Andre's case; namely, that there is an attempt to liberate the signifier as such from its obligation to relate to a signified. In this case, the signifier somehow becomes its own signified. The spectator's attention is directed at the piece itself, and there is no encumbering meaning outside of the work. The only meaning is what the piece is, and it is unfolded by the emphasis on the process of its making (or, as in the case of the " Prop " pieces, on its structure). Serra has made different " Splash " pieces in which the hot liquid metal was projected at the angle formed by the meeting of two planes (in some cases it is the floor and the wall of a room, in others just two pieces of metal), where it instantaneously solidified, preserving the record of all the energy necessitated by the projection. The form of the finished piece, including the smallest details, serves as evidence of the pure result of the simple actions (melting and projecting) that were performed upon the material. When the lead is left in the angle, without being removed, the actions performed do not attempt to impose any order upon the material; the place imposes its own order. In other instances, when Serra " uncasts " the lead and puts it upside down on the floor, next to other uncast splashings, he demonstrates the possibility of performing a simple " ordering "action for the sake of opposing order and disorder, natural and manmade. These same concerns appear in *Cutting, Base Template,* but conversely; in this case, as in the Pasadena Museum piece, material is placed on a plate in a simple order, and it is the action performed (the trimming of everything that is wider than or overlaps that piece) which creates the disorder. The cut elements fall on the floor in a random dispersion. The process of cutting is both evident and essential. It is the raison d'être of the piece. Because the process does not imply any particular dimension, the piece can be made in any scale, according to the dictates of the material, but independent of any human, anthropomorphic scale.

Serra's most recent pieces accentuate the importance of knowledge as well as that of the body's motion around and through the works. His Canadian land pieces, in particular, are determined by the nature of the terrain in which they are placed. For instance, a rectangular steel plate 24' x 8' is half buried in a hill, whose declivity is in the proportion of 8' x 24'. The place is cut at ground level. What is seen equals what is unseen; the cut edge is a profile of the ground, and the piece becomes information about itself as well as about its place. In other works created during the same summer of 1970, the landscape of the hills is accentuated in such a way as to perturb the spectator's perspective and sense of horizontality. Serra makes perception a discomforting rather than a reassuring experience; for, upon entering the area surrounding his works, the spectator becomes physically aware of the nature and forces of matter.

KEITH SONNIER

Of all the artists presented in this book, Keith Sonnier is perhaps the most subtle, a quality which, in recent times, has taken on a relatively bad connotation in art and art criticism as it is often mistakenly associated with decorativeness or even painterliness. The following quotation indicates how rapidly sensibility changes. Robert Pincus-Witten wrote in the October, 1969 issue of *Artforum* that " what [Sonnier has] been attempting to show is that the latex, the flocking, the neon, the rags, the cheese cloth were... substances analogous to the painter's palette." On the other hand, Rosenquist, six years earlier, made his *Tumbleweed* with almost similar materials, and it was considered one of his least painterly works. Sonnier, however, is not engaged in a purely " physical " direction. Instead of asserting the " what is, is," principle, which is one of the main issues of contemporary art, he presents pieces that are at the limits of pure being and " artistic " being. That thinness, fragility, lightness, and transparency should be associated with the delicacy of painterliness, discloses more about the nature of painting than about the nature of these qualities themselves. We have been so conditioned by the subtleness of painting that we can no longer see something that is not heavy and rough without associating it with this discipline. The same problem exists in respect to technology; strobe lights, amplifiers, and other such devices are so firmly established as theatricality that it is difficult to dissociate them from an aura of gimmickry as well as from a naive fascination with modernity, which has inspired so much " sociological " criticism. The rejective-reductive attitude has been essential in order to rid art of all tendencies that placed the art object on a level of reality different from that which simply exists. Sonnier is attempting to experiment in order to reintroduce into art some of the elements that had been rejected without, however, returning to the " artificial " mode of pre-Minimal art. It is in these terms that his work should be viewed.

Sonnier's flocked-latex wall pieces, done in 1968, were a successful answer to this problem. They were beyond painterliness because they were entirely determined by the simple process of putting the latex onto the wall, of flocking it, and of peeling part of the surface away from the wall. Aesthetic choices had no place in these works because their structures were determined solely by the set of physical conditions chosen by the artist. Moreover, the fact that part of the surface was peeled off and the rest attached to the wall made it evident that Sonnier was not dealing with the abstract space of painting, but with a given real space. The delicate, fragile, and ephemeral qualities of these wall pieces are not symbolically attained because of the artist's virtuosity, as they would be in the case of painting. Rather, they are the qualities that we generally ascribe to materials, such as flocking or thin layers of latex. The question of delicacy is a psychological one. It depends only upon the spectator's way of relating to what he sees. Seen as paintings, surfaces similar to those of Sonnier's wall pieces (such as the surfaces of Antoni Tapiès's paintings, for instance) give an impression of weight, massiveness, and strength, whereas they are perceived as fragile in Sonnier's natural situations.

There is a greater ambiguity in some of Sonnier's mixed-media works of 1968-69 in which he combines neon tubes with variegated, sometimes diaphanous, pieces of cloth. The relationships of one element to the others and the absence of ratio for the "composition," prevent them from being seen as materials in space and tend to relegate them to the realm of the three-dimensional collage. The interesting aspect of these works is the employment of neon, which is casual compared to a technology-oriented one. Nauman, Serra, Mario Merz, and a few other contemporary artists have occasionally used neon in the same manner, but it is Sonnier who has given the most consistent demonstration of the possibilities of this new medium. The 1960's witnessed a shift in attitudes toward technological devices and media. The rationalistic (and the self-satisfied, Occidental, optimistic) meaning of art's previous attempts to deal with technology and science gave way to a casual, nonrational, and sometimes "weird" appropriation, originated mainly by the electronic and pop music revolution. Sonnier is not fascinated with technology as such. He simply uses it without trying to camouflage its functional aspects; light sockets, electric cables, and transformers are not only apparent, but are part of his pieces. They are placed where they functionally belong. Sonnier has executed some neon pieces that have a remarkable degree of presence, mainly because there is nothing gimmicky about them. Light appears in them as what it is, a phenomenon, fluid energy. Late in 1969, he went even further in this direction by handling light as material and by making it interact with other kinds of light and with large sheets of glass.

Sonnier's most recent works, such as those shown in Eindhoven, Holland, or at the 1970 Whitney Annual in New York City (notably a pair of speakers on the rooftop of his building) are a synthesis of his early flock wall pieces and his experiments in neon. This is because they retain the concern for place and sensorial stimulation (the tactility of the flock pieces) and the deliberate use of technology, which characterized the later ones. A term other than "environment" should be found to define his three rooms at the Eindhoven exhibition. His intent was not to create a new visual field surrounding the spectator, but to place him in a space altered in such a way as to provoke new conditions of sensorial stimulation. In one of these rooms, two army projectors facing each other reflect themselves endlessly in two large and two small mirrors, creating an in-between zone of high-density light that becomes almost palpable. In another, the spectator's notions of density and perspective as well as his sense of touch are affected when he walks through the room. Large cubic volumes spread with pink fluorescent powder are lit with black light, thus losing their massiveness, while only the pigment catches the light. Before making this last work, Sonnier had experimented for months with different kinds of lights. He worked with soft volumes and spatial positioning, recording all the manipulations — which constitutes a performance in itself — with videotapes in which he attempted to use all the possibilities of this medium. The third Eindhoven structure dealt with sound, and so did the Whitney piece. Sonnier placed two speakers with amplifiers and feedback on the roof of his downtown building, catching the intensity of the street and traffic noises and transforming them into a continuous sound of varying intensity. Experienced from the street, even as far away as half a mile, it was like a quick, high-pitched vibration coming from nowhere. The experience was so disquieting that the work was sabotaged three times. In all of these recent works, Sonnier has used technological media functionally to affect the patterns of our system of relating with the physical world in a way that is similar to what can be achieved with drugs. Deprived of certitudes, the spectator faces a situation in which he has to re-align himself with reality or another reality and to re-invent his own new certitudes.

BRUCE NAUMAN

"Examination of physical or psychological response to simple or even oversimplified situations which can yield clearly experienceable phenomena."

BRUCE NAUMAN, "Notes and Projects," *Artforum,* December, 1970.

Linguistics has demonstrated that the analysis of a given language can reveal the complete mental structure of the people who use it. Benjamin Lee Whorf, in *Language, Thought and Reality,* quotes the Nootka word *tl'imshya'isita'itlma,* which condenses the whole concept of the English sentence " he invites people to a feast." Whereas the English-speaking mind needs four different words to define something, the Nootka simply adds five suffixes to the root *tl'imsh* (boil, cook), and whereas the structure of the English sentence is divisible into subject and predicate, the Nootka word follows a completely different logic, accentuating the result first and then the agency and the manifestation (boiled-eaters-go-for-he-does). This rather striking example of two different ways of intellectually dealing with the same event and with the same reality shows that, between the world and our mind, there is a whole system that we take for granted, but which is actually an arbitrary one, instinctively chosen and accepted by our civilization.

Word games, puns, and visual puns are the short circuits in this system, and it is not surprising that they have fascinated artists such as Duchamp or Johns, who have essentially tried to question this system. Among the questioners is Bruce Nauman, who illustrated the expression "from hand to mouth" in one of his early pieces by actually casting that part of his body stretching from hand to mouth. But Nauman comes at a time when art has abandoned the artificial limitations of the canvas or of the art object, and therefore he has been able to extend his questioning in several directions, including performances, films, videotapes, and "sculptures."

Probably one of today's most unpredictable artists, Nauman sees himself as having "overlapping ways of going about his work" (interview with Willoughby Sharp, *Arts Magazine*, March, 1970). He has a logic of his own, which is not too far from a child's prelogical mental structure. One of the key articulations of this type of logic is the question, "what can be done with, or what action can be performed upon, that particular thing?" This thing can be a word, a material, his face, his body, a spectator, a space, or anything. What is of primary importance is the experimental dealing with it: "I remember," said Nauman, "making lists of things you could do to a straight bar: bend it, fold it, twist it; and I think that's how the performance piece finally came about, because it was just the progression of action, standing, leaning, etc... which I carried out." Typical of this concern is Nauman's 1967 *Flour Arrangement,* a work that was a systematic exploration of the "different things to do" to a pile of flour in his studio each day for over a month. In *Making Faces,* a 1968 hologram piece in which his own face is used as a material that is deformed in various ways, one finds the same kind of inventory of all that can be done with or to something. It is as if Nauman wanted to show the multiple ways of physically dealing with it, notwithstanding what one is *supposed* to do with it. What is common to all of these creations is the intentional ignorance of any preconceived idea about how one should deal with reality, that is the ignorance of an accepted system of relationship with reality. This approximates the work of some contemporary musicians, such as Phillip Glass, who takes one short musical sentence and "manipulates" it until the listener's senses of rhythm, time, and melody are completely perturbed.

Permeating almost all of Nauman's work is another concern, namely, the forcing of the order of material into a new order. This creates a situation that is often the opposite of the one that was expected. In his early pieces based upon the process of casting, the inside becomes the outside; in the "John Coltrane" piece, the polished, mirrorlike face of a steel plate is put on the ground, facing it. Or else, in some of the "Performance Corridors," the spectator goes toward a television screen on which he can see his own body walking away. One of the most successful pieces based on this principle is *Two Rooms: Empty, Sealed and Private* (1970). One room is open to the public and one is completely sealed. Each has a video monitor and a camera, but the image that appears on the screen of the open room comes from the camera panning the sealed room and vice versa. In another piece, the spectator touches a wall on one side of a room and hears the sound on the other side (*Touch Piece*), thus perceiving the opposite of the expected result of his action. The artist's control over the situation is essential to these pieces about which Nauman has said that the problem was to "make a participation piece without the participants being able to alter your work." His intent works on the way a spectator psychologically and physically relates to something, unlike most of art, in which the spectator is free to react the way he wants. By depriving us of what we normally expect, Nauman creates a feeling of frustration, which is the origin of the "perversity" that some wanted to see in his work, but beyond this frustration is a more important issue. As Marcia Tucker observed in "Phenaumanology" (*Artforum*, December, 1970), "sensory deprivation experiments have shown that only the essential information needed to identify a thing tends to be picked up from a surrounding group of stimuli." A good part of Nauman's work consists in depriving the spectator of this "essential information" or in feeding him with surrogate information, thereby making him suddenly aware of all the other stimuli and forcing him to find his way around them.

The main achievement of Bruce Nauman's works is to make us perceive, on the different levels with which he has dealt (from conceptual to purely physical), the existence of a communications system between us and the world. His work confirms what experimental psychology has discovered, namely, that man had to "invent" a language of words, images, concepts, behavior, and body motion through which he could relate to his environment. Being "invented," these forms of language are the result of an "unconscious choice." They are exclusive of other forms of language and might be adequate only in one kind of environment. By slightly altering this environment, Nauman makes evident the inadequacies of our forms of language and forces us to find new systems of relationships with a changing reality.

Modern art is a continuation of an Occidental artistic tradition that first lost its ties with religion during the Greek Classical Age. Before, as well as in some other civilizations, the two formed man's most universal system of communication. Medieval art returned to the preclassical roots through an infusion of nomadic art-rituals from the barbaric invasions. However, since the Renaissance, the diagram of art history looks like a pyramid gradually rising from its primitive base and elevating itself toward a more and more refined abstraction.

General evolutionist theories, and especially Hegel's form of idealism and Nietzsche's Apollonian-Dionysian dialectic, have influenced art historians and critics to such a degree that it seems that late nineteenth century art and early twentieth century art is an almost direct consequence of these widely popularized ideas. A pyramidal view of art history tends to confirm an evolutionist aesthetic, each movement coming as a new level in the elaboration of the monument of history. But there is no sustained proof that it is in the nature of art to be evolutionary and to follow such logical rules as those of dialectics. Rather, further examination tends to prove that it is only the dominance of rationalism in Occidental culture that has produced such a type of art.

In *The Making of a Counter Culture,* Theodore Roszak predicts "that in the coming generation, large numbers of students will begin to reject this reductive humanism, demanding a far deeper examination of that dark side of the human personality which has for so long been written off by our dominant culture as 'mystical'." However, he also warns against the superficiality of some of the forms this new religiosity has taken. In many cases, the attempt to live according to another type of civilization is more a question of life style than an in-depth change in the Weltanschauung. The same can be said about art: fetichistic use of raw materials such as wood, ropes, rusted iron, or cloth has become the art mode among many minor artists, revealing a general desire to return to a primitive notion of art. But only a few have succeeded in going beyond problems of form and style into the primitive soul. The real issue is the breaking of a whole tradition of thought that has created a gap between intellectual experience and life experience, a gap that does not exist in the societies that have succeeded in integrating everything within one unified realm of experience. This is not only an issue for artist, but for everybody, because our civilization has reached a Stage

in which, as R. D. Laing pointed out in *The Politics of Experience,* "we do not need theories so much as the experience that is the source of theory."

When everybody believes that he, as a part, is able to relate by himself to the whole, art merely offers intellectual or sensual satisfaction. But when the finite individual senses the impossibility of relating alone to the infiniteness of the universe, art can be of vital necessity. It can rediscover its original function, namely, the dealing with the individual and collective experience of life in the universe. Space, Energy, Gravity, Scale, Time, Boundaries, Death — before having been absorbed by our intellectual categories — are the subjects of the very basic relation of man to his reality. They represent a field of motivations toward which artists are increasingly returning.

Joseph Beuys and Mario Merz, among the artists discussed in this book, are the ones who most cogently represent this attempt of art to rid itself of Cartesian intellectual structures. Both face nature and reality without preconceived definitions, without system or frame. Their art is a form of inquiry, a search for new ways of dealing with reality. (In a different manner, a sculptor such as Nancy Graves pursues a parallel goal through her manipulations of the mental image of the camel and of the shamanistic hangings.) Beuys's pieces and Happenings have ritualistic properties. They communicate something that passes directly from the senses to the unconscious. Unlike that of Beuys, Mario Merz's art is not expressive but analytic. His analysis, however, is less rational than intuitive. Searching for hidden structures in nature, he uses a methodology that is close to the one of alchemy, based as it is on repeated experiments without preconceived frames. His rediscovery of the Fibonacci, a medieval, pre-Cartesian law encountered in nature, is an example of his concern with an understanding of reality beyond all positivist explanation.

JOSEPH BEUYS

"Sculpture," says Joseph Beuys in an interview with Willoughby Sharp (*Artforum*, December, 1969), "must always obstinately question the basic premises of the prevailing culture." What is meant here is less political than metaphysical: through art, man has a chance to assert his freedom against all sorts of determinisms that society tends to impose upon him. Beuys is therefore not only in opposition to the capitalist system and its limiting values, but also to Marxism, which sees human life in terms of socio-economic conditions, and even to Freud's mechanistic view of the human mind. For him, teaching is one of the major aspects of his work. Essentially, it consists in showing his students new alternatives to all the systems imposed by our culture, and in emphasizing the truly creative faculties.

Art consists in the making of or in the changing of forms. But Beuys gives it a philosophical meaning. Form is the essential nature, the distinctive quality of something; it is what differentiates one thing from another within the continuum of unformed matter. Thus, any conscious and free change, or creation, of the essential nature of anything is an artistic activity, "the formation of a thought is already a sculpture" and "even peeling a potato can be art" (ibid.). His work proposes art as an action, a view that he shares with other members of the Fluxus group, whose members were among the first artists to promote Happenings in the early 1960's. They show a constant concern for provocation and anticonformism. Where Beuys differs from the rest of the Fluxus group is in his greater independence from a Dada or a Surrealist spirit, which has now become just another aspect of the accepted culture.

Unlike most contemporary artists, Beuys does not separate form from content. He always insists upon the expressiveness of what he does. At a time when message is being questioned in art, he is searching for a new vocabulary of sensation, for a new kind of language. This is what gives his work a ritualistic undertone. Performances like *Iphigenia* (Frankfurt, 1969) have something of the quality of a magical incantation. In *How to explain paintings to a dead hare* (Düsseldorf, 1965), the artist, with his shaved head and his face covered with grease, is almost like a warlock. There is a theatricality in these events that is not always convincing.

Where Beuys comes out strongly is in his approach to materials. With his wide concept of form, he is able to deal with any kind of material and to transform it into something that affects the spectator physically, intellectually, or emotionally. Beuys has used such diverse things as wax, grease, fat, felt, wood, metals, cloth, rope, loudspeakers, tape recorders, skeletons, dead and live animals, objects (boxes, pianos, air pumps, chairs, fences), electric lights, chemicals, and straw as elements of his vocabulary. No qualitative difference is made between real elements, images, materials, gestures, sounds, or physical phenomena. Everything is part of the all-encompassing language that he aims to create.

The faculty of abstraction is the property of intelligence, and language is generally based on this faculty. Abstraction, however, also means removal from reality; a word or a symbol is what we can detach from whatever its meaning encompasses. It has a time of its own, or rather, we consciously take it away from the flowing of time. Beuys's attempt is to create a vocabulary that speaks directly to the senses, a concrete vocabulary whose signs would be engulfed in time. Materials that deteriorate, fat that slowly melts, sounds, and living animals are juxtaposed with more permanent things, as in life. If the different structures of reality are a pure product of chance, as scientists, and specifically the biologist Jacques Monod believe, the language of Joseph Beuys is nothing else but a restructuring of reality according to an individual's need for expression. As much as possible, this restructuring is made in complete creative freedom, that is, notwithstanding all the nature-made or society-made existing structures.

The effectiveness of Beuys's language is largely based upon memory — both the memory of the different meannings we have learned to attach to things, and the one of the sensations experienced in the contact with them. In every one of his works, there is a constant interplay between what we remember and what we see, which comes close to the Surrealist way of isolating something from its natural context. Beuys, however, does not provoke the poetic encounter of isolated meanings in a foreign territory. He places the spectator in a situation that forces him to relegate what he has learned to the most obscure levels of memory and to face a new reality without any comforting previous knowledge. A time dimension is thus created in the mind, interfering with the piece's own time. The viewer's certitudes become no more real than those vague feelings of having already experienced an absolutely similar sensation or situation, which everyone has once in a while; amnesia and memory constantly interfere with each other.

Beuys's bid for cultural freedom has allowed him to transgress stylistic boundaries in his art. Although style and, on the superficial level of appearances, forms are not his main concern, he has played an important role in contemporary art by enlarging the existing possibilities. He has made a large use of soft materials as in Anti-Form, created works that in some ways anticipated Arte Povera, combined technology and raw materials in an approach close to Nauman's, and has repeatedly used his own body in performance situations as merely another artistic material. Other works, such as his *Felt Corner* or *Set III,* happen to be resolving spatial problems with the effectiveness of Minimal Art, and his *Fettecke* (fat pressed into the corners of a room) are informative about themselves in much the same way as Process Art is. Finally, by presenting his teaching as his principal work of art, Beuys has come close to Conceptual Art. But, throughout this diversity he manifests a complete disdain for art-history statements; he does not aim for aesthetic discovery, and he is not afraid of going back and forth between styles (occasionally, he makes drawings that look almost medieval). His diversity demonstrates his ambition to create a language that is as large as it can possibly be, a linguistic system that would come close to the numeric system imagined by Jorge Luis Borges, in which every number would have its own individual name without any relationship to the other ones. To a world whose structure is imposed on man, Beuys rebuts with a somehow demiurgic creation of a world that has the meaning that he, as a free individual, wants it to have. We too have this freedom, and, in this respect, it is true that the message of Beuys's teaching is the most important aspect of his work.

MARIO MERZ

"I search for Energy that flows, freed from the shackles of rhythm like the music of India."

MARIO MERZ

The aspects of reality that we see have very little to do with what reality is. Infra-red photography, for instance, makes it possible to take a picture of a past event. Beyond what our eye sees, there are hidden energies and structures about which we have only very theoretical and abstract notions. The world, as Mario Merz sees it, is a continuum of things and phenomena whose structures appear and disappear. In order to calm his anxiety, man has searched for a way of imposing an order on this fluctuating reality through positivist science. However, the proposed solutions have deepened the crisis by separating us from instinct and basic sensations. Mario Merz has used different techniques, ranging from handicraft to technology, and a wide range of materials, such as wax, clay, iron, neon, wood, cloth, and glass, to create situations in which things reveal their natural order. His pieces do not reveal anything about himself. They are not expressive, but uncover structures that have a poetic quality, as opposed to the structures that science has imposed upon reality, dynamic ones as opposed to static ones.

There is in his work a patience and a discretion that show his will not to force anything upon nature and to wait until it starts speaking about itself. His approach is supple, and he is prepared to adapt to the flexibility of his material. On one of his "Igloos" (a shape that he has been exploring since 1966) he quotes a sentence by General Giap: "If the foe concentrates itself, it loses ground; if it scatters itself, it loses strength." He comments thereupon by explaining that "the idea is round... If you follow the sentence you will get back to the beginning, and you will see how it winds itself, how it calms down. There is no clarification, no logic, no progress. It is a contained dynamic force." Merz's art is one of contemplation, but of a particular kind. It is not a contemplation that seeks harmony or beauty; it is a permeability toward the forces, energies, and ungraspable laws of reality. There is a certain accepted vulnerability and fragility, which is reflected in the materials Merz uses and in his quiet way of facing and experiencing what the intellect tends to reject as chaotic. Merz does not counter or interrupt the developments of this chaos. Instead, he uses the strategy of a judo player and redirects some of the emerging energies so that the spectator may participate in their mystery.

In 1968-69, Merz systematically explored the forest around Turin, Italy, looking at the peculiarities of the different spaces between the trees. After becoming familiar with these "negative spaces," he began to enclose them by wrapping cloth around coupled trees so that he could fill these spaces with liquid wax. When uncast, the block of wax retained the record of even the most minute formal characteristics of the spaces, which were virtually frozen at the particular moment in time at which they had been defined by the slow growth and changes of the trees. In this way, a process of change is stopped and transposed into another process of change, that of the soft piece of wax whose details are slowly erased by time. Through a simple act in which he respects the integrity of the materials and of the processes, Merz thus allows a set of formal, specific qualities to go from one continuity to another and from emptiness into sculptural mass.

Over two years ago, Merz began working on his *Fibonacci Series*, and created several pieces based on this mathematical series discovered during the Middle Ages by the monk Fibonacci. It is in fact a progression obtained by adding 1 to 1, 1 to 2, 2 to 3, 3 to 5, 5 to 8, 8 to 13, and so on. Geometrically, the series defines a perfect spiral. It includes all dimensions between zero and the infinite, accelerating its progression the more it tends toward the infinite. Another interesting thing about it is that, as Merz has experienced and verified himself, it acts as a structural guideline for nature in the growth of plants, the ramification of branches on a tree, and in other phenomena. But his interest is not a pseudoscientific one emphasizing some very precise law; it is rather a way of communicating the mystery of a hidden structure that can potentially encompass all dimension and all speed: the jump from the forthy-ninth to the fiftieth number (12,586,269.025) of the series being 4,807,526,976 times *faster* than the jump from one to two.

When shown in the actual space of a gallery or of a museum, the progression of the series does not have any undertones of a scientific demonstration. The numbers are just there, seemingly unexplainable. "A number," wrote Merz, « can be only one thing and nothing else; written in neon, it means this single number and nothing else, written in this particular way and no other. Neon is an object, but the fact that electricity flows through it renders it less an object." The numbers are like milestones in a system that includes the infinite; they are the only apparent concentrations of energy of a mental-poetic space that is open to all the possibilities, and which interacts with, and confronts, the actual limited architectural space.

The series is both precisely defined and entirely open, a fact that rendered it particularly appealing to an artist who had rejected the arbitrariness of subjective expression as well as the security of preconceived, rational systems. In Merz's experience of facing chaos without guidelines, the Fibonacci series parallels the "final meaning" sought by mystics; it rules the order of things without enclosing them in a man-made system.

Since the nineteenth century, art has been undergoing a process of accelerated changes. Aesthetic theories developed and were replaced by new ones at a pace faster than the public's taste and understanding could develop. The notion of avantgarde became a criterion in itself, based upon the knowledge and the overcoming of past achievements. But, despite the validity of the intent, it soon contributed to the widening of the distance between the artist and the public. In order to support and to promote avantgarde art, a whole structure had to be created; galleries, critics, and later, museums, formed a system that efficiently supported artistic experiments by exposing the artists to the few people who were able to appreciate their work. The nature of this system was determined by an art that required a sophisticated cultural background and whose aim was to reach the individual in his home.

The major changes that occurred in the art of the late 1960's merit special attention in view of their consequences upon the relationship between the artists and the public. The fundamental redefinition of art that occurred at this time did more than merely change forms within an accepted system; it challenged the system itself.

Today's art tends toward both a higher degree of theoretical complexity and a more immediate and effective direct contact with the viewer. Artists are now analyzing and redefining art as only a specialist in a limited field would do, and the aim of their research is the creation of an art powerful enough to reach even an unprepared public. To reach the cultivated individual in his home is no longer the concern of contemporary artists, who are creating works that exist by themselves, free from cultural conditioning, and to which anybody can go.

Walter De Maria and Michael Heizer have very little in common, except that they are both transgressing the limits of the accepted artistic system. On the most obvious level, they have bypassed this system by making large-scale pieces in the outdoors and by actually linking the value of the pieces to the value of the land on which they are built. To do this they had to deal with real estate agencies and engineering companies rather than with galleries and museums. But what is more important is that their art, even when suitable for the artistic system as it now is, does not require the understanding of the artistic tradition to be appreciated; rather, it is necessary to forget completely what one knows about art in order to experience their works. This is evident in all of De Maria's pieces which require that the viewer go through all the levels of his cultures in succession until he reaches the simple and universal truth of the work. De Maria manages to have the cultivated spectator reject all his knowledge. Heizer, on the other hand, prefers to base his art upon his own premises, which no longer refer to tradition. In both cases, the layman and the specialist become equals when they view the piece, and no cultural background can help the experience of the piece. Because of this, De Maria's and Heizer's art is, despite its remoteness, essentially a popular one.

The next few years will be decisive and crucial for the future of art. After having kept art exclusively for themselves and for a few specialists, artists are now ready to open it to a large public. While Conceptual Art is pursuing the tradition of a formal analysis of art and is trying to educate a public who has less and less access to the complexities of modern aesthetics, the more physical works of the artists I have presented insert themselves directly into reality. They offer a life experience rather than a codified aesthetic experience. Artists, after having long attempted to express in a visual language the reality of Cézanne's *Montagne Sainte Victoire*, have finally chosen to build their own mountain, which everybody can climb. Just as a structure had to be created to support the tradition of avantgarde art, a new structure will have to be found for this even newer art.

WALTER DE MARIA

" Se fait-on pas à tout? deux jours après la tonte,
Le mouton aguerri ne ressent plus le frais;
S'il peut rire, chanter, siffler, faire les frais,
C'est que le perroquet se fait vite à la chaine
Qui—lui qui sait vieillir comme vieillit un chêne
Quand nul n'est au persil des mets ou son bec mord
Le rive à son perchoir et l'y rivera mort;
L'envieux
Se fait aux profondeurs du grand vide celeste
Où la lumière court sans jamais le franchir."

RAYMOND ROUSSEL, *Nouvelles Impressions d'Afrique*, Chant 4.

Because of his unique use of the French language, Raymond Roussel is impossible to translate literally. The subject of these few verses is man's ability to get used to something, literally, "to make oneself to," just as "the sheep gets used to being shorn, the parrot to being chained to his perch until death, the envious one to seeing somebody else's success, or the astronomer to seeing the immense emptiness of the sky." The thirteen verses themselves are caught between triple parentheses, as if to prevent the reader from "getting used to" them, or, as if the whole commentary could be three times dismissed because it is irrelevant to what cannot be expressed. Despite the fact of his inevitable death, the parrot "can laugh, sing, whistle, make himself elegant." Such also is the system we use to prevent ourselves from seeing reality.

The work of Walter De Maria is centered around similar problems. Successive aspects of his pieces prevent us from seeing their very simple content. They are often shiny, polished, and elegant; some make sounds; some repeat the spectator's image by mirroring him; some are out in nature. His works refer to Minimal Art, to Conceptual Art, to Kinetic Art, and to Earth Art; yet all these qualities are only secondary aspects of his work, referring mostly to problems of forms and styles.

Walter De Maria's art requires the spectator to go beyond what is immediately apparent. In his early drawings, only the blank surface of the paper is apparent until one comes very close to it. From a distance, the *Beds of Spikes* look like Serial-Minimal artworks. De Maria's land works cannot be seen unless one goes to the desert. In each case, a passive art lover is offered a visual or an intellectual satisfaction that comes close to what other artists — Minimalists or Conceptualists — could propose, but this is of no importance for De Maria. What he is attempting is to restore the full power of revelation, which art has lost in our culture through a long tradition of symbolism and aestheticism. For instance, any artist who deals with death can only deal with the image of death or with the idea of death, and must do so in a language determined by the different conventions of art. Thus, when art speaks about death, it speaks inevitably in conventional terms and leaves the spectator unshaken because he is already *used to* these terms.

The evolution of artistic styles is partly due to this problem of avoiding all the idioms that have lost their strength through overexposure and cultural assimilation. Ultimately, however, the enterprise of changing styles eludes a definitive solution. De Maria has chosen to resolve the problem differently by creating an art that has several layers of meaning, all of which can be dismissed once the ultimate meaning is reached. Each layer has enough interest in itself to be culturally assimilated, so that it conceals the ultimate meaning that has to be faced as a real fact of life.

The *Beds of Spikes* are composed of five large industrially-produced stainless steel plates. They are as clean and simple as any other Minimal Art piece on which a series of sharp steel spikes has been attached. The number of spikes is in mathematical progression from one plate to the other, thus making each unit different from the other and interesting in itself and also as part of the series. This is an issue that has often been raised by Serial Art. In symbolic terms, the sharp spikes immediately evoke an art of deliberate cruelty which reminds the spectator of Surrealist aggressivity. Another interesting aspect of *Beds of Spikes* is the importance of its positioning since many different relationships can be established between the work and the different spaces in which it can be placed. All of these aspects are contained within the boundaries of art, and can be appreciated for what they are: the signs of a good understanding of the sculptural medium. The real experience of the piece, however, is far from an aesthetic experience. The spikes start to *work* when, walking between the different plates, one suddenly realizes that the spikes could easily kill anybody who lost his balance and fell upon them. The danger is no longer metaphorical; it is really there. Gravity is no longer a structural component of sculpture, it is a force powerful enough to kill.

The reason why *Beds of Spikes* are so efficient is that they catch the spectator when he is totally unprepared to face real danger. He has not had the time to get used to it and to formulate a psychological defense mechanism that would prevent him from facing his own fear. To create such situations, De Maria had to invent a real strategy based upon his knowledge of the spectator's psychological time mechanism. For the first few minutes one always expects anything or everything from a work of art. One is prepared to be shocked, aggressed, flattened, fooled, and one inevitably creates some protective barriers between the art and oneself. One stops protecting oneself only when the mind *grasps* the work, comprehending it enough to dominate it. At this point, the spectator is potentially vulnerable to everything unexpected. However, most works of art have nothing more to propose. De Maria's pieces are an exception because, up to this moment, they have intentionally kept their real meaning hidden.

A time element is essential to all of De Maria's works. In some, he is dealing with perceptual time; in others, with a real time continuity as in his movie *Hard Core* or in his musical compositions such as *Ocean and Drums*. In these two works, De Maria has created a very slow progression of intensity, which is boring enough to loosen one's defense mechanisms until the intensity suddenly becomes unbearably strong. One listens to the seemingly unchanging monotone rhythm of a set of drums, but in the background a sound of ocean waves has imperceptibly started. At a certain point, one realizes that the music is the sound of the ocean and no longer that of the drums. It is impossible to determine when the change actually occurs. In *Hard Core*, De Maria starts with very common scenes of country life, such as shots of cows, to bring us into the desert. From then on, the film consists of slow pannings of the desert and of the mountains in the background, taken at different times and from different locations within the same desert. The spectator gets progressively used to this landscape. He is forced to look closely at the earth, the arid vegetation, the colors of the sky. A few very brief shots of hands, feet with cowboy boots, and guns, serve as transitions between the different pannings without breaking the slow unfolding of time in the desert. Guns, all at once, start shooting; two cowboys are killing each other. The face of an Oriental girl appears on the screen. This is a typical example of De Maria's time strategy, which essentially consists in hypnotizing the spectator with slow information in order to make him receptive to the violent reality that will bring him out of his stupor.

Yet another example of De Maria's handling of time is manifest in *High Energy Bar*, a work that at first glance seems to establish a bridge between Minimal Art and Conceptual Art. It is a 14″ x 1½″ x 1½″ solid bar of polished stainless steel of which an unlimited edition was made. With each bar there is a certificate stating its ownership. Once given, the piece belongs *forever* to the person to whom it was given. The time factor involved here is the lifetime of the owner. Only his death can break the official tie between the work and himself. When described in simple terms, *High Energy Bar* sounds like an exciting idea. However, when one realizes that it is impossible to rid oneself of this bar — which also happens to be surprisingly heavy — there is a genuine feeling of anxiety. The stainless steel defies decay and death; one knows it will always be there, next to its owner.

One of the main aspects of De Maria's art is that it reminds us of the impossibility of understanding a piece of art without living with it for at least a certain time. This is true for any artwork, but most of the time there is not much more to discover in a piece afer the initial perception of it, because artists have not consciously explored this problem. De Maria, on the contrary, has directed all his work toward something beyond that which can be immediately perceived. To emphasize this point, he prohibits the reproduction of his works. To see his *Earthworks*, such as *Mile Long Drawing*, one is forced to go out into the desert. To get to the central meaning of any of his pieces, one is forced to pass through a whole intermediary stage of perception. Only under these conditions can art still have the power of generating a catharsis.

MICHAEL HEIZER

A preliminary analysis of the position of traditional sculpture in relationship to such problems as mass, time, size, and space will help situate Michael Heizer's own position.

In the past, sculpture was mainly a removable object. Even works that were meant to be part of an architectural ensemble could be (and actually often were) abstracted and removed from the whole, eventually to be sold and used as commodities.

This simple idea of removability has more complex implications. At first, there was a size limitation; only a certain scale in proportion to the human body's possibilities could be envisaged. The weight was equally limited. The mass of the sculpture was clearly distinct from the mass of the ground. The removability of the art object led artists to think that it could exist in its own particular time (the alleged immunity of art to the action of time) and in its own distinct space (which justified museums, galleries, churches, private apartments, and public parks as appropriate locations for this type of art). Sculpture became its own microcosm in which the different physical rules of nature were tentatively negated by the rules imposed by artists and other specialists. The illusion was that a volume was created independently from the existing real volumes, whereas sculpture was just the creation of a microcosm that was given a special status of existence by the aesthetic tradition; Judd's "specific objects" made this evident.

Within the frame of this briefly sketched, but basic, definition occurred relatively minor changes; different degrees of complexity, of simplicity, of abstraction, of precision in the details, and of alteration of the material. These were mainly matters of predominant tastes and aesthetic theories, which formed in their succession the history of art. Works that have a key position within this system are those that came as logical conclusions of a past step and allowed for the making of new steps; they are the so-called art-historical works. A work becomes truly historical, as opposed to "art-historical," when it does not refer to changes within this limited system and retains its strength outside of this system, bypassing the intermediary of the history of art. Such works are independent of the evolution of styles, and imply a complete redefinition of the premises on which "art" is based.

Michael Heizer's art is an art that clearly shows a different basic conception of mass, time, size, and space as compared to the conceptions on which 3,000 years of Occidental art are based. Whereas a few contemporary artists are merely "questioning" this tradition, he has simply taken other premises.

Dimension can be envisaged from the point of view of scale or from that of size. Scale requires constant relating to a standard. It is an intellectual way of comprehending dimension, based upon the possibility of dividing or of multiplying the standard unit of measurement. In architecture and in sculpture, man had become the standard; thus there was always the feeling of anthropocentrism. Most of man's creations are made according to his own scale, and when this scale is not evident he is struck by size. Size has nothing to do with man, except for his physiological inability to perceive sizes beyond his reach. Size is the intrinsic dimension of something. It is emphasized in the works that escape human scale, such as some of the Egyptian and pre-Columbian pyramids or the Stonehenge alignments, which are all based on astronomical scale. The perception of size tends to be disquieting in that it negates anthropocentrism. The size of the human body thus enters in direct relationship with the size of the piece, without the priority of the one on the other.

For instance, although Heizer's *Double Negative* can be measured in feet (1,600'), it asserts its size independently of scale. Or, if it does relate to scale, it is the scale of the Virgin River Mesa and not that of man, who is denied the possibility of comprehending the piece's dimension. In the catalogue of his exhibition at the Detroit Institute of Art, Heizer juxtaposed on a two-page spread the photograph of a work measuring 3″ x 1″ x 1″ with the photograph of a work covering an area of 450,000 square feet. The human scale (of which we are reminded by the view of two human feet next to the smaller work) is merely one of the intermediary scales between the two scales of the works.

Weight, being in proportion to size, is equally freed from the limitations imposed by the notion of a removable object. Not only can it be much more important, but it can also be separated from the finished piece itself. The weight of a Heizer piece cannot be compared to the weight of a sculpture that one can put on a scale; for it is not an isolated weight, but the measurement in tons of the energy that was needed to make the piece. In *Double Negative*, 240,000 tons of earth and rock were removed from the earth with dynamite and heavy machinery; in *Munich Depression*, 1,000 tons of earth were excavated; in *Fragmented-Depressed-Replaced Mass*, three blocks of 30, 52, and 70 tons of solid rock were moved by crane and transported for a distance of 60 miles from an altitude of 4,321 feet in the Great Basin desert plain of Nevada. Thus, the finished piece does not have its own weight; it simply exists as part of the earth's mass. This is the opposite of what happens with traditional sculpture, whose mass is always distinct from the mass of the ground, with a neutral base serving as intermediary between the two. In Heizer's case, the piece's own mass could at most be a negative mass; that is, the space that remains after the displacement of a mass. In terms of perception, the "presence" of a negative mass relates directly to the surrounding positive mass. As stated by Heizer, " aura has a density of extreme and unknown proportions." Negative mass also mnemonically refers to the prior positive mass and to the energy involved in its removal.

A work of Michael Heizer's can never be dissociated from its surrounding ground mass. His attitude toward the museum-gallery system is not so much one of theoretical rejection for socio-political reasons (as it is for many contemporary artists), but a question of practical necessity. None of his pieces exists in artificial spatial conditions, and none requires them. In terms of space, they actually tend to have difficult relationships with architecture; either they make the interaction impossible by almost disappearing, as in the Düsseldorf *Matchdrop*, or they aggressively assert themselves with a complete disdain for architectural space. In Detroit, this aggression was so violently felt that the city finally ordered the destruction of Heizer's 300-ton *Drag Mass Displacement*. When pure space is not available, the piece is not built; thus, the first version of *Drag Mass Displacement* was never built because of " difficulties in finding enough free ground " in New York.

Just as a Heizer piece does not require an artificial space, it does not require an abstraction from real time. We were used to seeing sculpture as something static in time, its forms having been fixed for eternity by the sculptor, as if he had intentionally closed his eyes on any possible alteration brought about by the effects of time. The spectator himself, seeing centuries-old sculptures, forgets that what he sees is not so much that which was created by the artist, but rather the result of the action of time upon materials. Heizer's *Circular Surface Planar Displacement* was erased by the first heavy rain; *Fragmented-Depressed-Replaced Mass* is in the process of being filled by mud; *Double Negative* is slowly crumbling and within a few millenaries it will be only a mere trace. All his works are integrated into the real time continuity, just as everything else is, including man. His works have different durations, ranging from a few days to a few millenaries, but these are only relative differences.

For Michael Heizer, sculpture is no longer a microcosm obeying the abstract rules established by the artist; it becomes a full part of the macrocosm. In the making of a piece, personal intervention is limited to the essential. Since true arbitrariness does not exist in the creation of a form or in the positioning of elements, the choice of sculpture was either to follow emotion-taste-expression-psychology-message oriented rules of composition, as a whole tradition of artists did, or simply to deal with the rules resulting from the nature of reality as does Heizer. The disposition of the matches in *Matchdrop* is entirely determined by the nature of the matches and the nature of the dropping. The drawing of *Circular Surface Planar Displacement* is obtained by the action of the wheels of a speeding motorcycle and is based upon the elementary geometry of two-dimensional positioning (inside tangential, intersecting, outside tangential, and outside nontangential are the only four possible placements of a circle in relationship to another circle twice as large in diameter). The *Munich Depression* has a depth and a diameter determined by actual conditions of vision and of perspective. Such compositional devices are not dependent on individual contingencies; they have a universal quality. In other pieces, such as the Detroit *Drag Mass Displacement*, the problem of composition is resolved by allowing an action entirely to define the final form of the work: the 30 tons. of rock was dragged by cables until it formed a 100-foot long and 2-foot deep depression, displacing 300 tons of earth.

In *Double Negative* the form initially is purely geometrical. It is then modified by the nature of the ground, which becomes a structural element in the making of the piece; for the form of the embankment obtained by the displacement of the earth is partly determined by the law of landslide, by the amount of earth, and by the declivity of the terrain. Such an attitude toward composition reinforces Heizer's refusal to abstract art from real time and natural space; it creates a necessary link between the material and the place.

Mainly for practical reasons, most of Heizer's pieces are located in very remote and isolated places, such as Coyote Dry Lake, Jean Dry Lake, Brack Rock, Smoke Creek, and Virgin River Mesa. This remoteness forced Michael Heizer to resolve the many problems involved in photographing his works. In order to avoid perspective distortion and give correct information about *Double Negative*, over 1,000 photographs of fragments were taken at right angles and equal distance, and were later glued on one plate. This montage of fragments represents a radically new means of reproduction, which is informative about the piece itself rather than about what one sees from one single viewpoint. For *Munich Depression,* a work based on central point vision, another approach was chosen; namely, a complete 360° view of the inside was made with nine photographs, taken at the inside base of the depression, making it possible to reproduce indoors the actual conditions of vision, abstracted from the other purely physical conditions. For these recent photographs, Heizer had an engineer build special projectors allowing full size, or *actual size*, projections to be made on the walls. Despite what they may seem to be, these are not simply reproductions of the works, but rather works in their own right for an indoor situation. In the development of iconology, the rock-projections (photographs of rocks in the land, untouched by the artist, with indications of mass and size) represent a step as important as Warhol's use of photomechanical serigraphy; for they are perfect examples of what today's inside-removable art can be. Thus, rather than reproducing his art in an indoor situation, or altering it to accommodate such limitations, Heizer uses the accepted idiom of art and renews it in order to render it efficiently informative about what his own art is. His drawings, prints, and indoor sculptures are equally convincing as contemporary removable art and as straight information about the outdoor pieces. They often have a very didactic purpose. The *.22 Drawing* is a good example. To make it, a roll of paper for industrial use was pierced by bullets and placed in a 17″ x 17″ x 46″ box of heavy industrial steel covered with a thick, bullet-proof glass top. It is a functional piece, lacking any gratuitous elements. It shows how traditional art forces the spectator to focus on a limited, protected, and artificial space. Essentially, the holes in the paper would have been the same if they had been made in the ground, but the piece displays them in the artificial context that is the proper realm of traditional art. In contrast, Heizer's own art deals with actual space.

The main reason for this new approach toward the making of art is efficiency. In the past, art became less and less powerful when removed from its specific context. On one hand, architecture was always physically more present in space; on the other, the acceleration of history developed into superpowerful forms of life that were much stronger emotionally than art ever was. It is not by chance that a good number of Heizer's works were built in Nevada, not far from Las Vegas, one of the most explosive centers of our civilization. To compete with a power like Las Vegas, art had to change fundamentally.

This text was written in New York during the months of April and May 1971.

The captions, chosen from the text were added in February 1972.   *Grégoire Müller*

DAN FLAVIN

SOL LEWITT

CARL ANDRE

ROBERT MORRIS

ROBERT SMITHSON

RICHARD SERRA

KEITH SONNIER

BRUCE NAUMAN

JOSEPH BEUYS

MARIO MERZ

WALTER DE MARIA

MICHAEL HEIZER

DAN FLAVIN

THEY JUST SIMPLY ARE.
THIS IS THEIR STRENGTH.

THE FLUORESCENT TUBES ARE INDUSTRIAL PRODUCTS. THEY ARE PUT ON THE WALLS BY ELECTRICIANS WHILE THE ARTIST REMAINS IN THE BACKGROUND.

ESSENTIALLY ALL OF THESE PIECES ARE THE SAME.

EXISTING
IN A PAR-
TICULAR
LOCATION
AT A PAR-
TICULAR
MOMENT
IN TIME.

39

NOT PUSHING LO-
GIC TO THE AB-
SURD BUT GET-
TING DOWN TO
THE ESSENCE OF
A PHENOMENON.

41

43

IN EACH PIECE, THE FLUORE-
SCENT TUBES ARE PLACED IN
A NEW SITUATION... IN EACH
CASE THE PERCEIVED PHENO-
MENON IS DIFFERENT.

THERE IS ONLY ONE WAY FOR AN ART-
WORK TO REFER TO SOMETHING REAL
WITH SOME DECENCY AND INTELLEC-
TUAL HONESTY; THAT IS, NOT TO REFER
TO IT AT ALL.

SOL LEWITT

ON WALLDRAWINGS

I wanted to do a work of art that was as two-dimentional as possible.

It seems more natural to work directly on walls than to make a construction, to work on that, and then put the construction on the wall.

The physical properties of the wall, height, length, color, material, architectural conditions and intrusions, are a necessary part of the drawings.

Different kinds of walls make for different kinds of drawings.

Imperfections on the wall surface are occasionally apparent after the drawing is completed. These should be considered a part of the wall drawing.

The best surface to draw on is plaster, the worst is brick, but both have been used.

Most walls have holes, cracks, bumps, grease marks, are not level or square and have various architectural eccentricities.

The handicaps in using walls is that the artist is at the mercy of the architect.

The drawing is done rather lightly, using hard graphite so that the lines become, as much as possible, a part of the wall surface, visually.

Either the entire wall or a portion is used, but the dimensions of the wall and its surface have a considerable effect on the outcome.

When large walls are used the viewer would see the drawings in sections sequentially, and not the wall as a whole.

Different draftsmen produce lines darker or lighter and closer or farther apart. As long as they are consistent there is no preference.

Various combinations of black lines produce different tonalities; combinations of colored lines produce different colors.

The four basic kinds of straight lines used are vertical, horizontal, 45° diagonal left to right and 45° diagonal right to left.

When color drawings are done, a flat white wall is preferable. The colors used are yellow, red, blue and black; the colors used in printing.

When a drawing is done using only black lines, the same tona-

lity should be maintained throughout the plane in order to maintain the integrity of the wall surface.

An ink drawing on paper accompanies the wall drawing. It is rendered by the artist while the wall drawing is rendered by assistants.

The ink drawing is a plan for but not a reproduction of the wall drawing; the wall drawing is not a reproduction of the ink drawing. Each is equally important.

It is possible to think of the sides of simple three-dimensional objects as walls and draw on them.

The wall drawing is a permanent installation, until destroyed. Once something is done, it cannot be undone.

SENTENCES ON CONCEPTUAL ART

1 Conceptual Artists are mystics rather than rationalists. They leap to conclusions that logic cannot reach.
2 Rational judgements repeat rational judgements.
3 Illogical judgements lead to new experience.
4 Formal Art is essentially rational.
5 Irrational thoughts should be followed absolutely and logically.
6 If the artist changes his mind midway through the execution of the piece, he compromises and the result repeats past results.
7 The artist's will is secondary to the process he initiates from idea to completion. His wilfulness may only be ego.
8 When words such as painting and sculpture are used, they connote a whole tradition and imply a consequent acceptance of this tradition, thus placing limitations on the artist who would be reluctant to make art that goes beyond the limitations.
9 The concept and idea are different. The former implies a general direction while the latter are the components. Ideas implement the concept.
10 Ideas can be works of art; they are in a chain of development that may eventually find some form. All ideas need not be made physical.
11 Ideas do not necessarily proceed in logical order. They

may set one off in unexpected directions but an idea must necessarily be complete in the mind before the next one is formed.

12 For each work of art that becomes physical there are many variations that do not.

13 A work of art may be understood as a conductor from the artist's mind to the viewers. But it may never reach the viewer, or it may never leave the artist's mind.

14 The words of one artist to another may induce ideas chain, if they share the same concept.

15 Since no form is intrinsically superior to another, the artist may use any form, from an expression of words, (written or spoken) to physical reality, equally.

16 If words are used, and they proceed from ideas about art then they are art and not literature, numbers are not mathematics.

17 All ideas are art if they are concerned with art and fall within the conventions of art.

18 One usually understands the art of the past by applying the convention of the present thus misunderstanding the art of the past.

19 The conventions of art altered by works of art.

20 Successful art changes our understanding of the conventions by altering our perceptions.

21 Perception of ideas leads to new ideas.

22 The artist cannot imagine his art, and cannot perceive it until it is complete.

23 One artist may mis-perceive (understand it differently than the artist) a work of art but still be set off in his own chain of thought by that misconstrual.

24 Perception is subjective.

25 The artist may not necessarily understand his own art. His perception is neither better nor worse than that of others.

26 An artist may perceive the art of others better than his own.

27 The concept of a work of art may involve the matter of the piece or the process in which it is made.

28 Once the idea of the piece is established in the artist's mind and the final form is decided, the process is carried out blindly. There are many side-effects that the artist cannot imagine. These may be used as ideas for new works.

29 The process is mechanical and should not be tampered with. It should run its course.

30 There are many elements involved in a work of art. The most important are the most obvious.

31 If an artist uses the same form in a group of works, and changes the material, one would assume the artist's concept involved the material.

32 Banal ideas cannot be rescued by beautiful execution.

33 It is difficult to bungle a good idea.

34 When an artist learns his craft too well he makes slick art.

35 These sentences comment on art, but are not art.

A THING
NEVER
FAITHFULLY
REFLECTS
ITS IDEAL
CONCEPT.

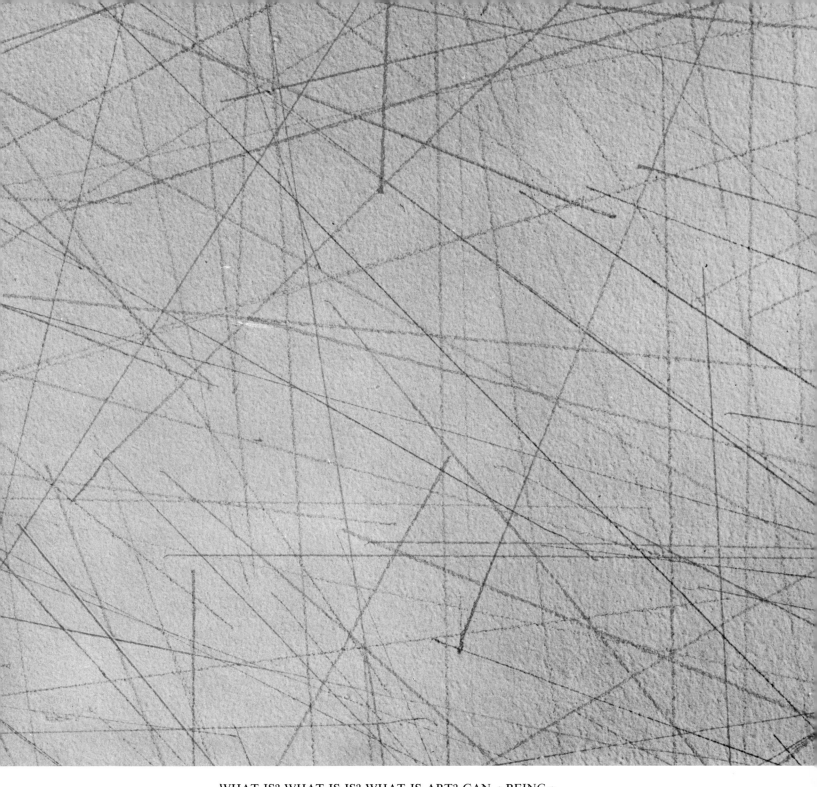

WHAT IS? WHAT IS IS? WHAT IS ART? CAN « BEING »
BE SEPARATED FROM « BEING HERE AND NOW »?

A RISK CONSCIOUSLY FACED WHEN DEALING WITH THE DUALITY OF ART.

MATERIALIZATION IM-
PLIES IMPURITY... THE
ACCEPTANCE OF EVERY-
THING ONCE THE CON-
CEPT, THE « DECISION »,
HAS BEEN CHOSEN.

TO CONTROL THE PARASITIC MECHANISM OF FORM.

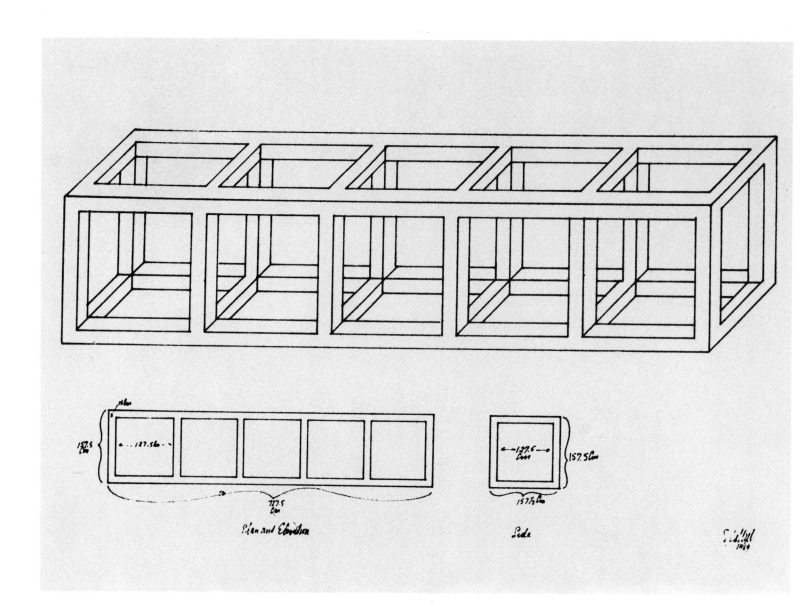

ENCLOSING AND ENCLOSED ARE COMBINED. DIMENSIONS TAKE ON AN-
OTHER MEANING ACCORDING TO THEIR SCALE. SHADOWS CHANGE THE
PIECE AS THE OBSERVER MOVES AROUND IT.

55

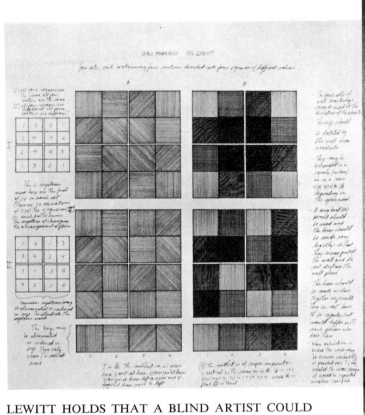

LEWITT HOLDS THAT A BLIND ARTIST COULD
PERFECTLY WELL MAKE ART.

56

THE UNEXPLORED
AREA BETWEEN
THE WORLDS OF
IDEAS AND OF
REALITY.

CARL ANDRÉ

THE FOLLOWING PHOTOGRAPHS OF MATERIALS,
AS THEY HAPPEN TO HAVE BEEN ABANDONED IN
THE STREETS OF NEW YORK CITY, WERE TAKEN
UNDER THE INSTRUCTIONS OF THE ARTIST.

IF SCULPTURE
RISES IN SPACE,
IT RUNS THE RISK
OF BECOMING JUST
AN ARTIFICIAL
CONSTRUCTION.

SIMPLE ADDITION OR RANDOMNESS.

THEY PROPOSE
A REAL EXPE-
RIENCE...
SCRATCHES,
TRACES OF
HUMAN CON-
TACTS, RUST,
AND OTHER
MARKS OF
TIME ARE ALL
RECORDED ON
THE PIECE.

ANDRÉ HAS REFUSED TO GIVE ART A
SPECIAL STATUS OF EXISTENCE.

QUESTIONING
THE CONCEPT
OF IDENTITY.

ROBERT MORRIS

HOW WE
PERCEIVE IT
BECOMES MORE
IMPORTANT THAN
WHAT IT IS.

A RAW PHYSICAL FACT CANNOT BE PERCEIVED
WITHOUT GETTING PROCESSED IN THE MIND
ACCORDING TO A EUCLIDEAN CONCEPTION
OF SPACE.

*PLACEMENT BECOMES CRITICAL AS IT NEVER WAS
BEFORE IN ESTABLISHING THE PARTICULAR
QUALITY OF THE WORK.*

Robert Morris (October, 1966)

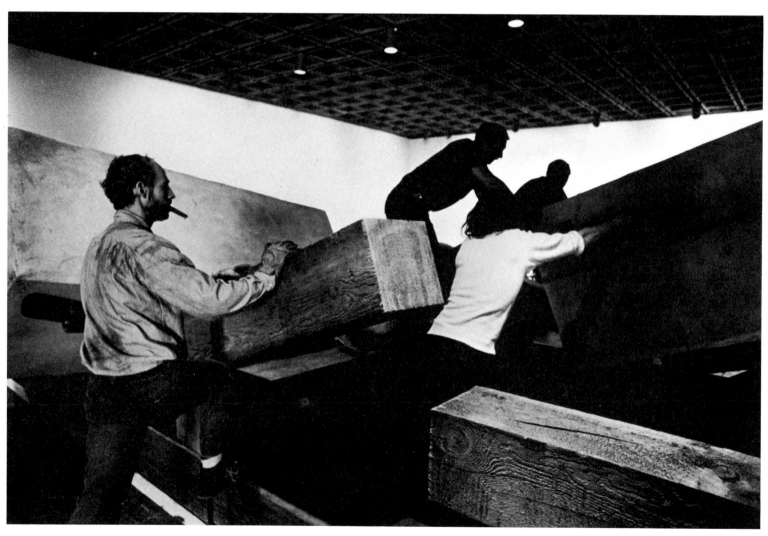

THE « SELF » AS A SUBJECT DISSOCIATES ITSELF
FROM THE « SELF » AS AN OBJECT.

THE ACKNOWLEDGEMENT OF THE PROCESSING OF
THE VISUAL DATA INTO INTELLECTUAL CATEGORIES.

MANY MASKS OF WHAT HIS WORK REALLY IS.

BEYOND
MORRIS'S
HANDLING
OF MATE-
RIALS AND
OBJECTS,
THERE IS A
HIGHLY
CONTROLLED
HANDLING
OF THE
SPECTATOR'S
MIND.

THE
« ANTI-
ORDER »
ATTITUDE
TOOK
ON AN
IMPRESS-
IVE DI-
MENSION
AT THE
WHITNEY
MUSEUM. ▶

ROBERT SMITHSON

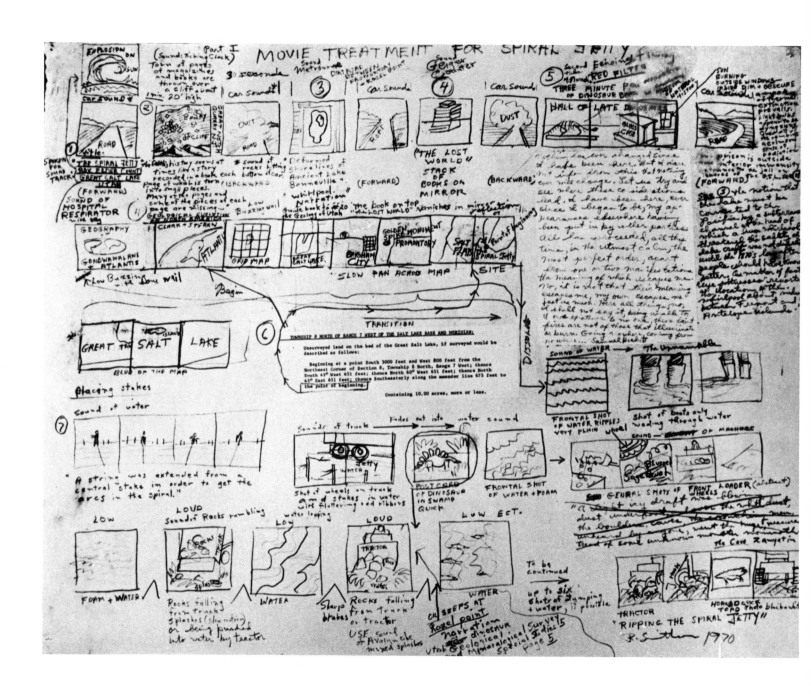

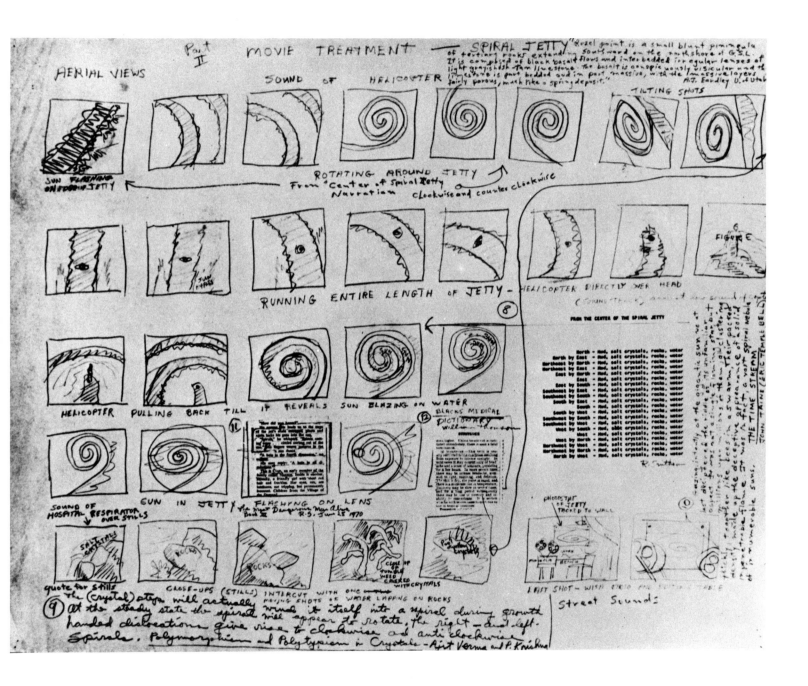

81

« SPIRAL JETTY. » GREAT SALT LAKE, UTAH.

THE PERCEP-
TION OF THIS
PIECE IMPLIES
THE UNDER-
STANDING OF
A DEVELOP-
MENT IN TIME.

THE SPIRAL
AND THE LAKE
EXIST ON THE
SAME LEVEL
OF REALITY.

AN AESTHETIC CHOICE AS WELL AS A DOOR OPEN TO THE « OCEANIC ».

SUCH A
METHODOLOGY
IS SUITABLE
BECAUSE IT
TERMINATES
IN A MORE
PHYSICAL RESULT.

CHALLENGING THE SENSE OF LIMITS AND THE
RELUCTANCE TO SUSPEND THE BOUNDARIES
BETWEEN « SELF » AND « NONSELF ».

ITS GEOMETRIC CONFIGURATION IS A SYMBOL FOR
EVOLUTION (GEOMETRIC: FROM EARTH AND
MEASURE).

COATLICUE SAID: YOU HAVE NO FUTURE, AND CHRONOS SAID: YOU HAVE NO PAST... BUT COATLICUE CONCLUDES: YOU DON'T HAVE TO HAVE EXISTENCE TO EXIST.
— *ROBERT SMITHSON* (1969)

CATEGORIES
ARE SHAKEN,
EXPOSING
DEEPER STRUC-
TURES OF UN-
DERSTANDING.

RICHARD SERRA

TO ROLL	TO HOOK	TO MARK
TO CREASE	TO SUSPEND	TO EXPAND
TO FOLD	TO SPREAD	TO DILUTE
TO STORE	TO HANG	TO LIGHT
TO BEND	OF TENSION	TO REVISE
TO SHORTEN	OF GRAVITY	TO MODULATE
TO TWIST	OF ENTROPY	TO DISTILL
TO TWINE	OF NATURE	OF WAVES
TO DAPPLE	OF GROUPING	OF ELECTROMAGNETIC
TO DAPPLE	OF LAYERING	OF INERTIA
TO CRUMPLE	OF FELTING	OF IONIZATION
TO SHAVE	TO COLLECT	OF POLARIZATION
TO TEAR	TO GRASP	OF REFRACTION
TO CHIP	TO TIGHTEN	OF SIMULTANEITY
TO SPLIT	TO BUNDLE	OF TIDES
TO CUT	TO HEAP	OF REFLECTION
TO SEVER	TO GATHER	OF EQUILIBRIUM
TO DROP	TO ARRANGE	OF SYMMETRY
TO REMOVE	TO REPAIR	OF FRICTION
TO SIMPLIFY	TO DISCARD	TO STRETCH
TO DIFFER	TO PAIR	TO BOUNCE
TO DISARRANGE	TO DISTRIBUTE	TO ERASE
TO SHAVE	TO SURFEIT	TO SPRAY
TO OPEN	TO SCATTER	TO SYSTEMATIZE
TO MIX	TO COMPLEMENT	TO REFER
TO SPLASH	TO ENCLOSE	TO FORCE
TO KNOT	TO SURROUND	OF MAPPING
TO SPILL	TO ENCIRCLE	OF LOCATION
TO DROOP	TO HIDE	OF CONTEXT
TO FLOW	TO COVER	OF TIME
TO SWIRL	TO WRAP	TO TALK
TO ROTATE	TO DIG	OF PHOTOSYNTHESIS
TO SMEAR	TO TIE	OF CARBONIZATION '67-'68
TO FLOOD	TO BIND	
TO FIRE	TO WEAVE	
TO IMPRESS	TO JOIN	
TO INLAY	TO MATCH	
TO LIFT	TO LAMINATE	*SERRA*
TO CURVE	TO BOND	
TO SUPPORT	TO HINGE	TO CONTINUE

IN THE 1960'S, SCULPTURE MOVED AWAY FROM A SELF-CENTERED INTIMISM AND BEGAN TO REACH INTO ACTUAL SPACE.

RATHER THAN FOLLOW THE PATTERNS THAT WE INSTINCTIVELY RECOGNIZE AS NORMAL OR ACCEPTED, SERRA REDISTRIBUTES THE ELEMENTS.

MATERIALS,
PROCESSES,
THOUGHT
MECHANISM,
TIME, HORI-
ZONTALITY,
VERTICALITY,
COMPOSITION,
WEIGHT,
DISORDER,
PERSPECTIVES,
GESTALT,
KNOWLEDGE,
STRUCTURES
PHYSICA-
LITY... ARE
SOME OF THE
ASPECTS
UNDER WHICH
THESE PIECES
MAY BE CON-
SIDERED

THE INSTICTIVE MAPPING OUT OF A TERRITORY IS NOT THREE-DIMENSIONAL, BUT IS SYNTHETIC OF ALL THE EXPERIENCES WITHIN THIS TERRITORY.

THE EXPERI-
ENCE OF THEIR
SHEER WEIGHT
AND POTENTIAL
TO COLLAPSE.

MULTI-SENSORIAL PERCEP-
TION OPENS THE WAY FOR A
NEW APPROACH TO SPATIAL
PROBLEMS.

THE PIECE BECOMES
INFORMATION ABOUT
ITSELF.

WHAT IS SEEN EQUALS WHAT IS UNSEEN.

KEITH SONNIER

Mirror Act

I
Body Mind

II
Body Life

III
Body State

Keith Sonnier

SONNIER IS NOT FASCINATED WITH TECHNOLOGY AS SUCH. HE SIMPLY USES IT WITHOUT TRYING TO CAMOUFLAGE ITS FUNCTIONAL ASPECTS.

 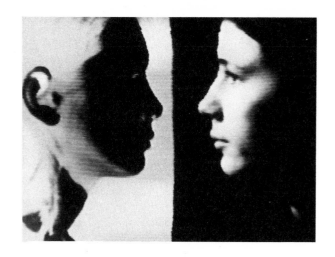

 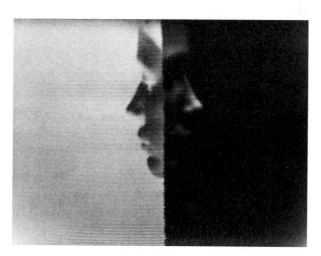

DEPRIVED OF CERTITUDES, THE SPECTATOR FACES A SITUATION IN WHICH HE HAS TO REALIGN HIMSELF WITH REALITY OR ANOTHER REALITY AND TO REINVENT HIS OWN NEW CERTITUDES.

THE MANI-
PULATION
AND
SPATIAL
POSITIONING
OF THE SOFT
VOLUMES
BECOMES A
PERFOR-
MANCE IN
ITSELF.

108

BEYOND
THINNESS,
FRAGILITY,
LIGHTNESS
AND
TRANS-
PARENCY.

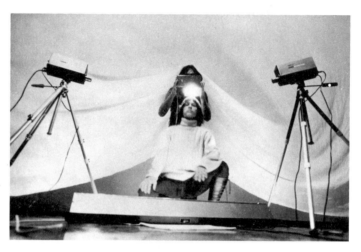

A SHIFT TOWARDS A
« WEIRD » APPROPRIA-
TION OF TECHNOLOGY
AND SCIENCE, ORIGIN-
ATED MAINLY BY THE
ELECTRONIC AND POP
MUSIC REVOLUTION.

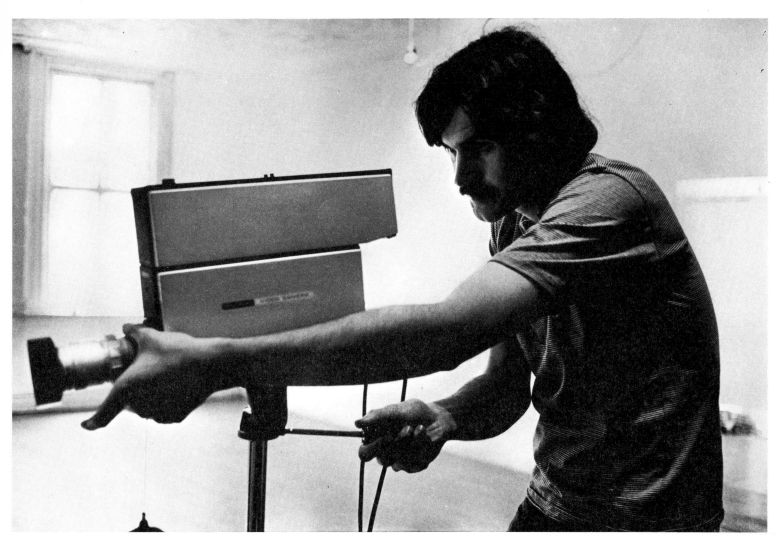

USING THE TECHNOLOGICAL MEDIA TO AFFECT THE PATTERNS OF OUR
SYSTEM OF RELATING WITH THE PHYSICAL WORLD IN A WAY SIMILAR
TO WHAT CAN BE ACHIEVED WITH DRUGS.

THUS LOOSING THEIR MASSIVENESS, WHILE ONLY THE PIGMENT CATCHES LIGHT.

THE INTENSITY OF THE STREET
AND TRAFFIC NOISES
TRANSFORMED INTO A
CONTINUOUS SOUND OF
VARYING INTENSITY.
(SABOTAGED THREE TIMES)

BRUCE NAUMAN

LACK OF INFORMATION INPUT
(SENSORY DEPRIVATION) → BREAKDOWN
OF RESPONSIVE SYSTEMS.
PROVISION OF INFORMATION WHICH IS SKEW
RATHER THAN CLEARLY REINFORCING OR CON-
TRADICTORY →
2 KINDS OF INFORMATION EACH OR WHICH TO
UNRELATED RESPONSE MECHANISM.
(SKEW LINES NEVER MEET AND ARE NOT
PARALLEL IN SPACE — BUT THEY CAN BE VERY
CLOSE TOGETHER OR VERY FAR APART).
WITHDRAWAL AS AN ART FORM?
SENSORY MANIPULATION
(AMPLIFICATION)
(DEPRIVATION)
SENSORY OVERLOAD (FATIGUE) DENIAL OR
CONFUSION OF GESTALT (VOLUNTARY — INVO-
LUNTARY)
INVOCATION OF PHYSIOLOGICAL
DEFENCE MECH.
EXAMINATION OF PHYSICAL AND PHYSIOLOGICAL
RESPONSES TO SIMPLE OR EVEN OVERSIMPLIFIED
SITUATIONS WHICH CAN YELD CLEARLY
EXPERIENCEABLE PHENOMENA.
→ PHENOMENA + EXPERIENCE ARE
UNDIFFERENTIABILITY.

Bruce Nauman

THE ANALYSIS OF
A LANGUAGE CAN
REVEAL THE COM-
PLETE MENTAL
STRUCTURE OF
THE PEOPLE WHO
USE IT.

BETWEEN THE WORLD AND OUR MIND THERE IS A WHOLE SYSTEM THAT WE TAKE FOR GRANTED.

FEEDING THE
SPECTATOR WITH
SURROGATE
INFORMATION,
THEREBY MAKING
HIM SUDDENLY
AWARE OF ALL
THE OTHER
STIMULI AND
FORCING HIM TO
FIND HIS WAY
AROUND THEM.

121

INVENTED FORMS OF
LANGUAGE MIGHT BE
ADEQUATE ONLY TO ONE
KIND OF ENVIRONMENT.

THE
ARTIST'S
CONTROL
OVER THE
SITUATION
IS ESSEN-
TIAL TO
THESE
PIECES.

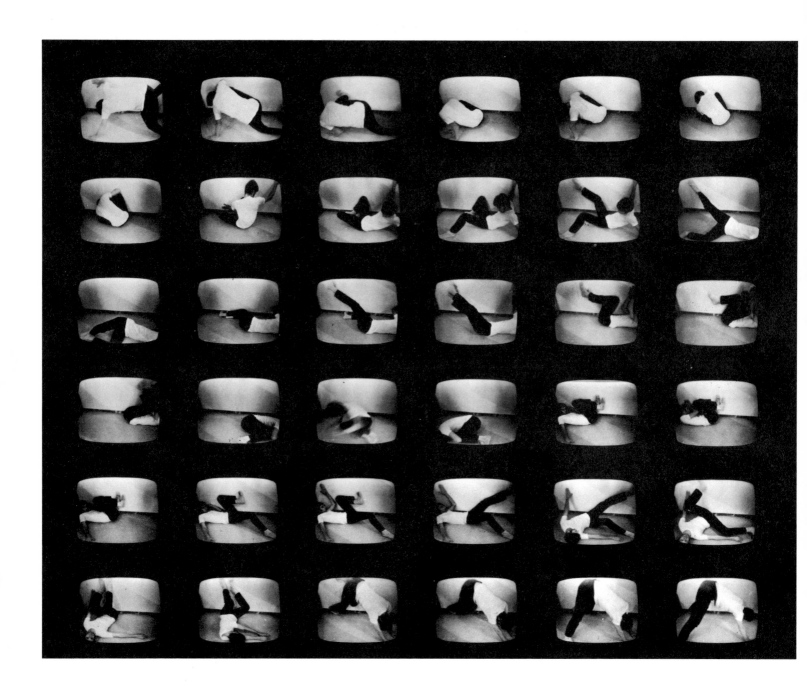

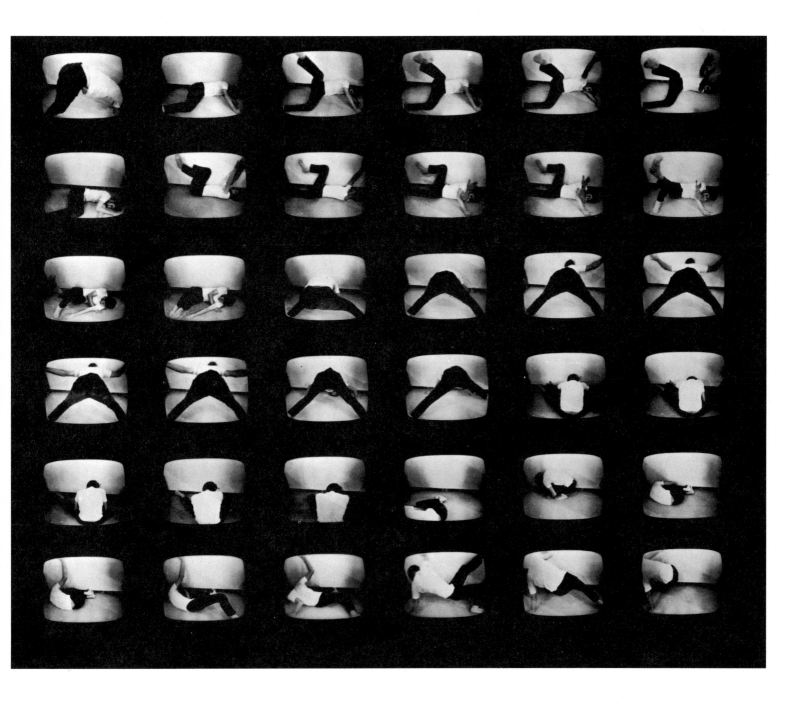

MAN HAD TO INVENT A LANGUAGE OF WORDS, IMAGES, CONCEPTS, BEHA-
VIOR, BODY MOTION, THROUGH WHICH HE COULD RELATE TO HIS ENVIRON-
MENT.

TO MAKE EVIDENT THE INADEQUACIES OF OUR FORMS OF LANGUAGE.

"...IT WAS JUST THE PROGRESSION OF ACTION, STANDING, LEANING, ETC...
WHICH I CARRIED OUT".   BRUCE NAUMAN 1970

JOSEPH BEUYS

i

O

Ǝ

A

∩ RFT

THÜR UND DIE ZIMMER
IN DENEN ICH GELEGEN BIN
GESCHLAFEN HABE
HIER IST NICHTS WAS ZU BEGREIFEN WÄRE
IHR KÖNNT MICH NICHT EINFACH IN DIE ERDE
KRATZEN

IHR SAGT DIE MENSCHLICHE NATUR SEI FÜR
DIE REVOLUTION NICHT GEEIGNET
WOHLAN VERÄNDERN WIR DANN DIE NATUR DES
MENSCHEN

Dies ist meine Axt
und dies ist die Axt von meiner Mutter.
J. B. 1963
Das ist nicht Ihre Schuld, was Sie gesagt
haben, aber dass man Sie gefragt hat.
Joseph Beuys
→
aus :   « Hauptstrom »

Joseph Beuys

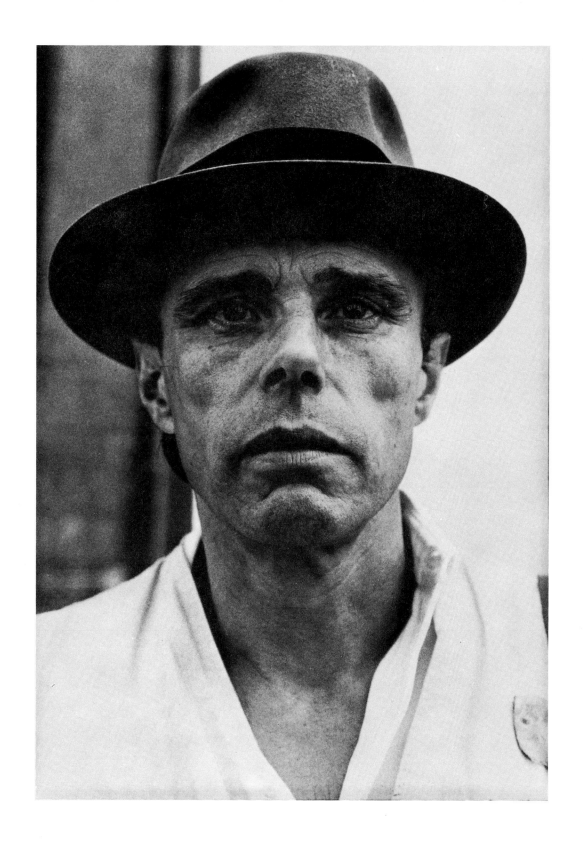

BEUYS'S BID
FOR CULTURAL
FREEDOM
HAS ALLOWED
HIM TO
TRANSGRESS
STYLISTIC
BOUNDARIES.

EVERYTHING IS PART OF THE
ALL-ENCOMPASSING LANGUAGE
THAT HE AIMS TO CREATE.

A CONCRETE VOCABULARY
WHOSE SIGNS WOULD BE
ENGULFED IN TIME.

MATERIALS THAT DETERIORATE, FAT THAT SLOWLY MELTS, SOUNDS,
AND LIVING ANIMALS ARE JUXTAPOSED WITH MORE PERMANENT THINGS.

A TIME DIMENSION IS CREATED IN THE MIND...
THE VIEWER'S CERTITUDES BECOME NO MORE
REAL THAN THOSE VAGUE FEELINGS OF HAVING
ALREADY EXPERIENCED AN ABSOLUTELY SIMILAR
SENSATION OR SITUATION.

THE DIFFERENT MEANINGS WE HAVE LEARNED TO
ATTACH TO THINGS, AND THE MEANING OF THE
SENSATIONS EXPERIENCED IN THE CONTACT WITH
THEM.

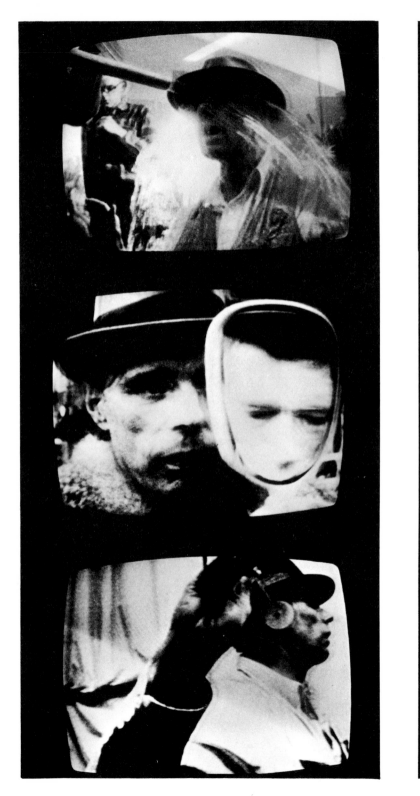

MAN AS A CHANCE TO ASSERT HIS FREEDOM
AGAINST ALL SORTS OF DETERMINISM THAT
SOCIETY TENDS TO IMPOSE UPON HIM.

AMNESIA AND MEMORY CONSTANTLY INTERFERE
WITH EACH OTHER. *COME SONO LONTANE QUEL-*
LE MONTAGNE. JOSEPH BEUYS (1971)

MARIO MERZ

SOMMARIO

1, 2, 3, 5, 8, 13, 21, 34, 55 uomini hanno mangiato. La proliferazione degli uomini è legata alla proliferazione degli esseri da mangiare e questi alla proliferazione degli oggetti prodotti poiché questi uomini sono operai di una fabbrica di Napoli.

Una cascata e il tempo

Cinque colonne nel mistero dei numeri.
1   1   2   3   5

Mario Merz

THE ASPECTS OF REALITY
THAT WE SEE HAVE LITTLE TO
DO WITH WHAT REALITY IS.

THE WORLD IS A CONTINUUM
OF THINGS AND PHENOMENA
WHOSE STRUCTURES APPEAR
AND DISAPPEAR.

MERZ'S
ART IS ONE
OF CONTEM-
PLATION,
BUT OF A
PAR-
TICULAR
KIND: IT
IS NOT A
CONTEM-
PLATION
THAT
SEEKS
HARMONY
OR
BEAUTY

144

IT IS A
PERMEA-
BILITY
TOWARD
THE
FORCES,
ENERGIES
AND
UNGRASP-
ABLE
LAWS OF
REALITY.

145

THE NUMBERS
ARE LIKE MILE-
STONES IN A
SYSTEM THAT
INCLUDES THE
INFINITE.

AN EX-
PERIENCE
OF
FACING
CHAOS
WITHOUT
GUIDE-
LINES.

147

IN ORDER TO CALM
HIS ANXIETY, MAN
HAS SEARCHED FOR
A WAY OF IMPOSING
AN ORDER ON THIS
FLUCTUATING
REALITY THROUGH
POSITIVIST SCIENCE.
HOWEVER, THE
CRISIS WAS
DEEPENED
LEAVING US
SEPARATED FROM
INSTINCT AND BASIC
SENSATIONS.

149

WALTER DE MARIA

MY DEALERS

The following 6 people have represented me and my work to the outside world in the 10 years of my professional career.

RICHARD BELLAMY

PAULA COOPER

ARNE EKSTROM

NICHOLAS WILDER

HEINER FRIEDRICH

VIRGINIA DWAN

I would like to thank them, for our past association and for representing me here, for I do not like to be photographed.

(THIS PHOTOGRAPHIC LAYOUT HAS BEEN DETERMINED BY THE ARTIST HIMSELF).

RELIGIOUS, SENSITIVE, GOOD

WARM, LOVING, HELPFUL

PROFESSIONAL, ELEGANT, INTELLIGENT

DASHING, FLASHY, WITTY

POSSESSED, ENERGETIC, CRAZY

MOODY, MYSTICAL, MINIMAL

Walter De Maria

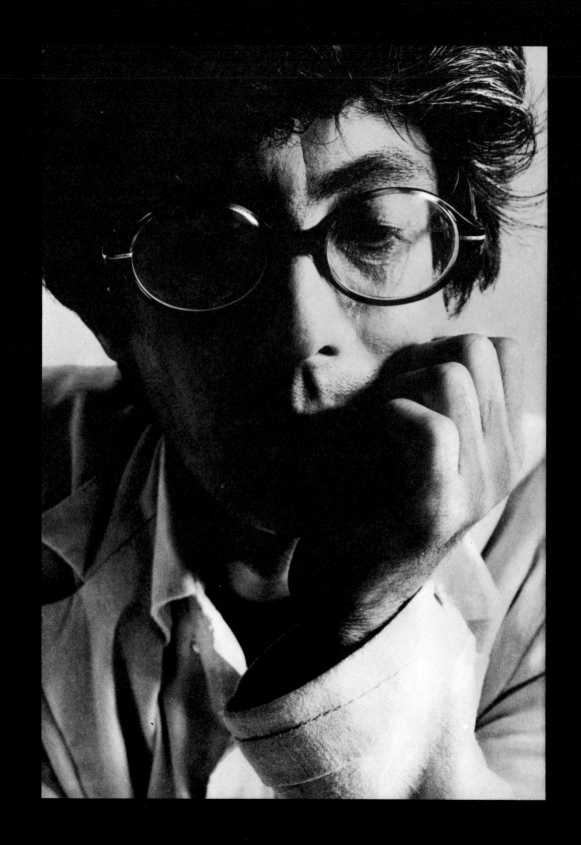

...coyotes, Silver Slipper, pumas, mesquite, scorpions, AEC research and t

phototroposis, quail, Ruth pit, carp, Tropicana, faro wheel, 87 land gov

speed limits, gila Monsters, eagles, manganese, Wagon Wheel, creos

herons, joshua, antimony, Hacienda, suicide table, Mint, hawks, greatest

diatomite, owls, petroglyphs, Flamingo, palace, 3885 registered brands,

cindercones, gold, tarantulas, razorbacks, chapparal, silver, Dunes, co

octillo, barite, Indian reservations, buckhorn, arch welding, coin-

International, geysers, pelicans, Landmark, timber rattlers, sand, titaniu

Circus-Circus, tufa, blackjack, seagulls, basalt, nuclear munitions stockp

Las Vegas, jackrabbits, Sands, bobcats, Harrahs, 1 member U.S. House o

Barney's, Mormon tea, Harvey's, silica, Folies Bergeres, Aladdin, frogs

Lear, juniper, kildeer, rodeo horses, cottonwoods, lizards, cattle, legalized

Sahara, wolves, Thunderbird, granodiorite, Mapes, borate, Lady Luck

r, baccarat, natural pyram kan o rats, mescal, squirrels, cultural

% ownership, hot spring ule sidewinders Great Basin, open

s, rhyolite, wild ses, Yucca Flat, slot machines, centipedes,

te transient population, Harold Club, uranium, black widows, copper,

lfur, mountain lions, Showboat, ard Hughes, tungsten, Frontier,

kes, gypsum, willows, playas, foxe Dese on rows, pine, Stardust,

Boulder Dam, roadrunners,

s, javelinas, cholla, bingo, county-optioned prostitution, yucca, turtles,

r Queens, six week divorces, molybdenum, Golden Nugget, drift shafts,

sentatives, Sierra Nevada (solid granite), sinkholes, bats, sage, mudflats,

al SST landingstrip, seven mile tunnel, The Strip, mackinaw, William

ng, only architecturally uniform U. S. city, feldspar, bombing ranges,

antelope.

DOUBLE NEGATIVE (1969-70) 1500' x 50' x 30'. 240,000
TONS DISPLACEMENT. VIRGIN RIVER, MESA,
NEVADA, U.S.A. LOOKING FROM EAST TO WEST.

NEGATIVE MASS MNEMONICALLY REFERS TO THE
PRIOR POSITIVE MASS AND TO THE ENERGY
INVOLVED IN ITS REMOVAL.

160

A DIFFER-
ENT BASIC
CONCEPT-
ION OF
MASS, TIME,
SIZE AND
SPACE
CHALLENG-
ING 3,000
YEARS OF
OCCIDENTAL
ART.

"AURA HAS DENSITY OF EXTREME AND UNKNOWN PROPORTION".
MICHAEL HEIZER

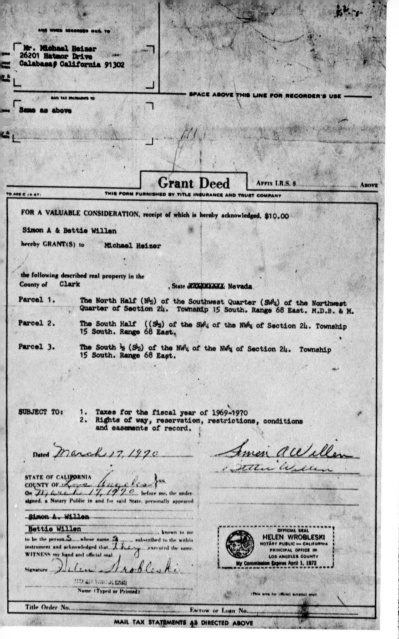

A NEW STRUCTURE WILL HAVE TO BE FOUND FOR THIS NEW ART. SCULPTURE BECOMES A FULL PART OF THE MACROCOSM.

30 TON GRANITE MASS, 28' x 4½' x 4'.

IN DETROIT, THIS AGGRESSION WAS SO VIOLENTLY
FELT THAT THE CITY FINALLY ORDERED THE
DESTRUCTION OF THE 300-TON DISPLACEMENT.
« DRAGGED MASS ».

« DISPLACED-REPLACED MASS » (1969) SILVER SPRINGS, NEVADA. THREE BLOCKS OF 30, 52, AND 70 TONS OF SOLID ROCK WERE MOVED BY CRANE AND TRANSPORTED FOR A DISTANCE OF 60 MILES FROM AN ALTITUDE OF 4,321 FEET IN THE GREAT BASIN DESERT PLAIN OF NEVADA.

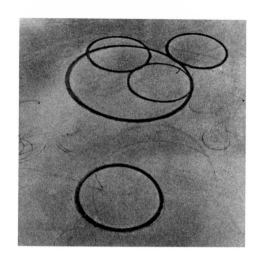

« CIRCULAR PLANAR DISPLACEMENT DRAWING »... ERASED BY THE FIRST RAIN.

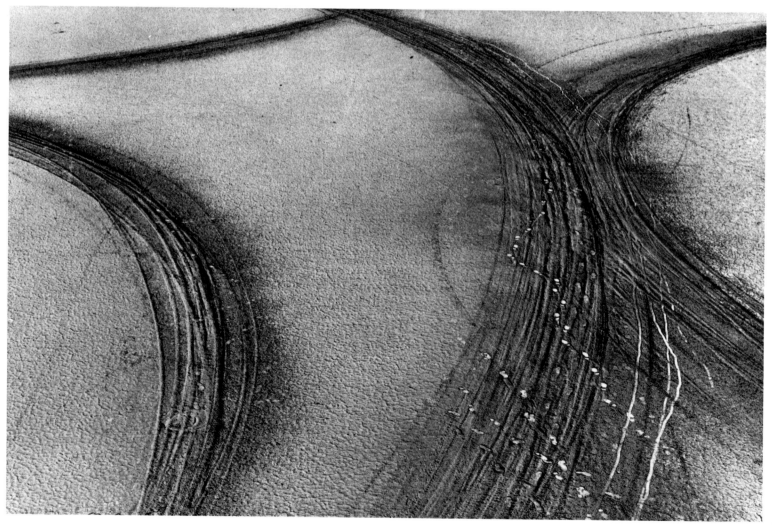

THE ONLY
FOUR POSSI-
BLE PLACE-
MENTS OF A
CIRCLE IN
RELATION-
SHIP TO
ANOTHER
CIRCLE
TWICE
AS LARGE IN
DIAMETER.

DIFFERENT
DURATIONS
RANGING
FROM A FEW
DAYS TO A FEW
MILLENARIES,
BUT THESE
ARE ONLY RE-
LATIVE DIFFE-
RENCES.

173

INDEX